Tales of a Virtuous Woman Wannabe

Tales of a Virtuous Woman Wannabe

Discovering in the Chaos That God Really Likes Me

Leigh Ann Northcutt

To Greg,
my love,
my partner,
my biggest fan,
and the subject of my best
material

Give thanks to the LORD,
for he is good;
his love endures forever.
Let the redeemed of the LORD
tell their story.

Psalm 107:1–2

Contents

10   A wife of noble character who can find?
      She is worth far more than rubies.

11   Her husband has full confidence in her
      And lacks nothing of value.

12   She brings him good, not harm,
      All the days of her life.

13   She selects wool and flax
      And works with eager hands.

14   She is like the merchant ships,
      Bringing her food from afar.

15   She gets up while it is still night;
      She provides food for her family
      And portions for her female servants.

16   She considers a field and buys it;
      Out of her earnings she plants a vineyard.

17   She sets about her work vigorously;
      Her arms are strong for her tasks.

18   She sees that her trading is profitable,
      And her lamp does not go out at night.

19   In her hand she holds the distaff,
      And grasps the spindle with her fingers.

20   She opens her arms to the poor,
      And extends her hands to the needy.

21   When it snows, she has no fear
      for her household,
      For all of them are clothed in scarlet.

22   She makes coverings for her bed;
      She is clothed in fine linen and purple.

23   Her husband is respected at the city gate,
      Where he takes his seat among the elders
                  of the land.

24   She makes linen garments and sells them,
      And supplies the merchants with sashes.

25   She is clothed with strength and dignity;
      She can laugh at the days to come.

26   She speaks with wisdom,
      And faithful instruction is on her tongue.

27 She watches over the affairs of her household
      And does not eat the bread of idleness.

28   Her children arise and call her blessed;
      Her husband also, and he praises her:

29   "Many women do noble things,
          But you surpass them all."

30   Charm is deceptive, and beauty is fleeting;
      But a woman who fears the
                  LORD is to be praised.

31   Honor her for all that her hands have done,
      And let her works bring her praise
                  at the city gate.

Introduction

I am a daughter of the South.

I'm not talking about the recent South of Paula Deen, Duck Dynasty, or Ricky Bobby and his nights in Talladega. I'm a descendant of the South that belonged to my grandparents, where temperatures were hot and air was unconditioned, when everything moved at a leisurely pace to hamper the progression of sweat that rolled down backs and dripped into shoes.

The metronome that sets the pace for my life clicks a slow beat. My thoughts ramble around a subject until they come full circle. Then they continue on for another stroll, making it nearly impossible to come to a quick decision. My steps tend to be unhurried. They move slowly through life so as not to bash my shins on the bits and pieces of the world I fail to notice because my thoughts are meandering about unattended. Even vowel sounds dawdle on my tongue, taking twice as long as needed to express themselves.

I am a master at putting off doing things. I'm pretty sure I am the official "pro" in procrastinator. I take pride in knowing just exactly how long I can wait to begin a writing project or clean my house or potty train my kids and still have the job done adequately before the final deadline or company knocks on my door or the first day of kindergarten. Since the time of my childhood chores, I have lived by the old saying "Why do today what you can put off until tomorrow? Because if you put it off until tomorrow, you can curl up with a good book today." In my life, that adage falls third in line of importance, just below "Love God and live" and "Raising children is like nailing Jell-O to a tree."

I know about raising children. I have reared five of them, along with one husband who emphatically refuses to grow up. Unfortunately, each time I thought I had parenting figured out, the Lord gave me a new child with an entirely different set of challenges, and I had to learn how to do it all over again. The one thing I can say for certain is that, for me, much of young motherhood was about simply surviving the day. I realized early that a mother must survive today because her precious angel-demons will need her, alive and well, to love them tomorrow.

I am a homemaker who has trouble making things homey. I am a less than enthusiastic cook who chooses new recipes based on the number of ingredients and how many pans will need to be washed at the end of the meal. I am a female with a short supply of femininity who does not own a pair of heels and thinks the painting of toenails is a tremendous waste of time.

I spent years wondering how to deal with the traditional church's version of the woman described in Proverbs 31. If you have studied the book of Proverbs, you know her as the Virtuous Woman. She is the wisdom of Beth Moore, the kindness of Mother Teresa, the initiative of Oprah Winfrey, and the domesticity of Martha Stewart rolled together into the body of a model and powered with the stamina of the Energizer Bunny.

Women like me love God and want everything He desires for them. But we approach life from a laid-back, domestically challenged point of view. How do we deal with the intimidating Virtuous Woman of God? How do we tackle the formidable standards set in the Proverbs 31 passage?

It is not easy. We tentatively approach them with more than a little angst and varying amounts of ineptitude.

But it helps if we can laugh about it . . .

1 I Took Up Sewing and Learned to Cuss

She enjoys knitting and sewing.
Proverbs 31:13 THE MESSAGE

Her hands work the sewing spindle.
Proverbs 31:19 ISV

During my first years of marriage, creative domesticity meant crawling onto my husband's lap at the end of a workday and dramatizing the whine that begged him to take me out for supper. I was working a minimum wage job and my husband was in law school, so we were as poor as the proverbial church mice. Despite my pleading, most days ended with me in the kitchen preparing my signature dish: spaghetti a la Ragu.

When my husband graduated and took his first job, I threw mine to the wind and declared that I was ready to take domesticity seriously. At the time, we were attending a church where most of the women had chosen to be full-time homemakers and stay-at-home mothers. To offset the lack of a second income, they had become masters of frugality and domestic arts. On Sunday mornings, the pastor's wife thawed a chicken, cut it into pieces (no pre-packaged chicken parts for her) and fried it for lunch while washing and hanging clothes to dry on the line in her backyard. All this was done before leaving for church to teach a Sunday school class.

I did well to find the time to shave my legs as I showered on Sunday mornings.

Those women were my introduction to the Virtuous Woman of Proverbs 31. They were wise and kind and had much to teach me about initiative and domesticity. In my mind, they wore handsewn capes and large VWs sequined to their chests. I became their official Wannabe. With those ladies as my mentors, I was sure to become a Super-Virtuous-Woman with an array of awesome domestic powers.

I had been cooking for a couple of years by that time and my husband had neither died of food poisoning nor left me for his mother. So I decided learning to sew would be my first venture into the life of a Proverbs 31 Woman. My friend Laura offered to teach me.

She said it would be easy.

She said there was nothing to it.

She said I would enjoy it.

She was wrong.

I was in over my head from my first step into the fabric store. We walked through the door and entered Laura's place in the world. She stopped to take in the sights and sounds of the store, breathing deeply to inhale the scent of the various fabrics that filled the shelves.

I took a dumbfounded breath beside her and exclaimed my dismay, "Day lands!" (an expression of emotion in the Northcutt family, to be used only in the most extreme of situations). The bolts of cloth extended as far as I could see. And I had to choose from them!

I have never been good at making decisions, and I was pretty sure we were going to be there all day.

It was then that I first heard Laura speak in tongues. At least,

I assumed it was tongues because it sounded like gibberish to me. Eventually, I realized she was not using the kind of tongue language Paul talks about in the Bible. Laura was speaking the unique language of the Proverbs 31 Virtuous Woman. With no one there to interpret, I was completely baffled.

"Something…chambray…something…rayon…a strange and confusing something…voile. What do you think?"

What did I think? Until that moment, I had thought chambray was a wine. I was pretty sure rayon would kill me. And voile? Wasn't that a little animal that traveled through mole tunnels and ate my mother's flower bulbs?

Evidently, my friend missed the dazed look in my eyes because she kept talking. "Let's just go with cotton…blah blah…double cloth…blahdy-blah…broadcloth…big, baffling blah blahs… chino or damask?"

Damask? Was that a question? For me?! She was going to have to speak English or ask somebody else.

"Wah, wah, wah…something about a bias…yada, yada, yada… cut on the cross-grain…[Are these even words?!]…serge the selvage edges."

At that moment, I prayed for the first time what was to become my theme prayer as a Virtuous Woman Wannabe, "Lord, help me! Lord, help me now!"

As I prayed, Laura dragged me through the store. We loaded a shopping cart with the things she assured me I would need as I learned to sew: fabric, patterns, thread, zippers, buttons, and a small tool, which was to become my best sewing friend—the seam ripper.

For the next few months, Laura patiently taught me to sew. It took six weeks to learn to thread the machine. It would have been easier to run electrical wiring through a nuclear power plant. When I could thread the machine, I worked on sewing a straight line. Then I practiced sewing a straight line. Then I drilled myself on sewing a straight line. Then I lied and said I could sew a straight line.

Laura did not like to waste time, so we didn't begin by making potholders or hemming handkerchiefs. Having recently learned I was pregnant with our first child, Laura suggested I begin my sewing lessons with a simple maternity top. It had no buttonholes, no zippers, no sleeves, and no shape. There were only a few steps from start to finish. The pattern instructions could have been written on a Post-it Note.

Laura said we should be able to finish the top in a day. Again, she was wrong.

It took significantly longer than a day. In fact, I think God may have had that top in mind when He made a woman's gestation last nine months. I ripped out a seam every time I sewed one. There were so many holes in the fabric, it could have been used as mosquito netting.

After a few months of Laura's coaching, I bought my own sewing machine and immediately went to war with it. Having survived the battle of the maternity top, I moved on to skirmish with the machine over pillows and bedding for a crib. The machine drew first blood. Literally. But I persevered and, in the end, the items held together. I placed them in my future son's baby bed. Since science had proven that newborns are basically blind, I hoped the bond between my child and me would be sealed and cemented before his vision developed and he awoke one morning to see that his mother was inept.

By the time my son was two, I had become a competent seamstress, but I was far from being the Virtuous Woman I wanted to be. Without Laura by my side, I began to vocalize the hostility I felt toward the act of sewing. "Crap!" which was perfectly acceptable in my home, stretched to "Crap, crap, crap, crap!" and then became the more questionable, "Crapfire!"

With the seeds of a potty mouth having been planted, a tentative "shhhhh . . ." was soon slipping through my lips. In due time, the "t" found its way out of my mouth and I found myself "sht"ing more and more often as I sat at my sewing machine.

Then the day came when I totally lost control. I was tackling the most difficult and most impressive of my sewing projects. Having completed a shirt and jumpsuit for my son to wear to church, I was working on a dress I would wear. The cuffs on the sleeves did me in.

As I put the cuffs on crooked, I felt an "i" rolling around in my chest. When the sleeves puckered, the vowel sound rose into my throat. I cut through a buttonhole…and there it was! The fourth letter erupted from my mouth to join the other three and this Virtuous Woman Wannabe had learned to cuss.

At that point, I reassessed my first attempt at becoming a Proverbs 31 Woman. It seemed that learning to sew had been counterproductive. So I gave it up. I quit sewing. Not because I hated every single second at the machine. Not because I loathed every stitch I had put in every garment. Not because my seam ripper had declared itself abused and overused and disappeared from my sewing box. I stopped sewing, burned my fabric, patterns, threads, zippers, and buttons, and ran over my sewing machine with a dump truck purely for my spiritual health.

At least, that is what I told my husband.

And I'm sticking to it with no-sew fusion tape.

Before I set fire to my seamstress aspirations and fudged an excuse about it, I asked God, who knew all there was to know about my VWW spiritual motives, if it was okay for a Virtuous Woman Wannabe to give up sewing. That question may surprise you. You may think it too trivial to put before the God of the universe. When I was young and thought I needed to prove my worth to a distant deity, I would have agreed with you.

I grew up in the Southern Baptist Church, the one that sits on the corner in the center of every small town in the Bible Belt of the United States. I left my imprint all over that building. My footprints can be found running through every hall and stairway. My handprints, mixed with generations of others, continue to rest on the rail into the baptistry. Crumbs that I dropped from hundreds of potluck dinner plates are probably still hiding in the corners of the basement. I wouldn't be surprised to find that song notes from my voice continue to hang slightly flat somewhere in the choir room. I'll bet my DNA can still be found on the water fountain. I slurped from that fountain from the time I had to stand on a stool to reach the spout until the day I stooped to get a drink in my wedding gown.

The pew that sits about two-thirds back on the left side of the sanctuary holds my bum print, which started small and spread with age. At 10:45 on most Sunday mornings of my childhood, I sat on that pew with my family. Dressed in our best duds, we sang from the 1956 printing of the *Baptist Hymnal*, accompanied by several women who served as church pianists. Mrs. Charlene Williams, to the best of my knowledge, sat in stockinged feet on the organ bench every Sunday from the day the church was founded in the late 1800s until a few years ago when the angel in charge of heaven's choir practice needed an organist and the Lord called her home.

From the pulpit of that church, I was introduced to the God who lives in heaven. I was taught how to learn about Him and encouraged to serve Him. But it was not in that building that I came to know how much He loved me. That happened in one of the dark places of the world. One day Jesus met me in a spot where I thought no self-respecting member of the Godhead would be. Because He sat down and wrapped His arms around me there, I learned that He is not a distant God. As a result of His mercy to me that day, I have walked the steps of my life's journey recognizing that He is with me everywhere, and I talk to Him about everything.

With no reservation about the triviality of the question, I asked God if it was okay for a Virtuous Woman Wannabe to give up sewing.

He said it was fine.

I don't think He had been particularly impressed with the fruits of my sewing labors.

2 Marching to the Beat of a Slow and Mellow Drummer

She gets up before dawn.
Proverbs 31:15 NLT

She works late into the night.
Proverbs 31:18 GNT

She does not eat the bread of idleness.
Proverbs 31:27 NASB

I read.

I read in my favorite chair. I read on the front porch. I read in the car. I read while I cook. I read while my husband watches dumb stuff on TV. I have been known to read at my kids' sporting events while pretending to watch them play ball.

It's an addiction. The fragrance of the pages draws me to the book. My hands shake a bit as I open the cover and crack the spine. No matter how many times I tell myself that I'm going to read only one chapter, I'm fated to a reading binge after the first paragraph. An insightfully-turned phrase sucks me into a story every time. A sympathetic character and a well-crafted plot bind me to it.

When my children were young, I turned pages in a fictional world while they wandered the house ignored and neglected. As a longtime reader, I learned years ago that I could read at least a hundred pages before most name-brand diapers turn to mush. Letting my kids go hungry for an hour or so would get me an extra three to four chapters.

Others are like me. Other readers spend their days craving a book fix; others also have volumes stashed in every corner of their homes and keep paperbacks hidden in their purses and pockets. Columnist and Pulitzer Prize–winner Anna Quindlen said, "Books are the plane, and the train, and the road. They are the destination and the journey. They are home." President John Adams said, "I read my eyes out and can't read half enough…The more one reads the more one sees we have to read."

I stand in the company of my fellow addicts and know that I am chief among these sinners. I admit that I have a problem. I also have my own 12-step addiction program to address it. When overcome with the need to read, I sneak away from my family and climb the 12 steps to my bedroom. I crawl to the far side of the bed with a book clenched between my teeth and hide there while I consume a few of its pages.

My name is Leigh Ann, and I am a read-a-holic.

Ironically, my fictional heroines never fall prey to the same addiction. They are women who have no trouble meeting the standards of the Virtuous Woman. They live with their families in worlds of industriousness. Just like the women on my refrigerator.

My husband gives me the same Country Seasons Calendar every Christmas. The calendar is a small thing, but my husband, who is generally clueless about choosing presents for me, is always sure it will please me. It hangs on my fridge where each month's picture paints a scene of family life from 150ish years ago.

In January, a team of matching horses pulls a sleigh of children up a country lane. The children, cocooned in flannel blankets, are laughing as they ride up the hill to a farmhouse where lamps glow in the windows to welcome them home. In May, a man stands behind a plow under the shade of a large oak tree. His shirt is drenched with sweat, and he fans himself with his hat as he surveys with a look of satisfaction the newly furrowed field that will support his family for the coming year.

Those images of life long ago appeal to me, but it is the pictures of the women that draw me to that calendar. In September, a woman stands in her kitchen, hot from the warmth of the wood-burning stove behind her. The pail, which I feel sure she used to milk the family cow before dawn that morning, sits on the floor by the stove. The knitting she will do late into the night lies in a basket in a chair by the door. With purpose in her arms, the woman is leaning over her table, kneading dough in a wooden bowl. I would bet my VWW membership pin that no drop of idleness is anywhere in her bread.

I'm not sure why I am so drawn to the women on my calendar. Maybe a part of me thinks they will step off the refrigerator and teach me their Virtuous Woman ways. Maybe. I hope their presence in my kitchen will inspire me to confront life with domestic purpose and work my way through the day at a swift pace. I only know that when I study the women in those paintings, I want to be like them. I think I should be like them.

Evidently, God disagrees.

While I was in my mother's womb, He formed my body. He molded each of my inward organs and gave my heart a beat. He counted the hairs as He placed them on my head and sculpted each of my fingers, placing a thumb in my mouth to comfort me even before I was born.

I believe that with the same painstaking gentleness God also formed my soul. Before I saw the light of day, I was made to delight in the color of the sky. Before I drew a breath, I was destined to savor a storm. With His brow furrowed and His tongue caught between His teeth in an expression of concentration, God sculpted the essence of me. (This picture is a product of my imagination. Don't look for it in your Sunday school literature.)

As much as the Virtuous Woman Wannabe in me would like it to be otherwise, God did not fashion me to be a Country Seasons Calendar Woman. He created me to be a woman who is intimidated by domestic purpose, who loses her way when the pace of life is hurried, and who will, often as not, burn the biscuits because pages of a book are still to be read. When I try to be someone other than me, I flounder like a fish out of water. I also rob Him of the chance to know and enjoy me as He created me.

So I won't be milking cows. I am allergic to them as well as the barns in which they live. I won't spend my evenings knitting. I have no more ability to knit than I have to sew. And odds are that the pace at which I work through my day will not pick up much. The Lord and I both know He did not create me to hurry through life.

I am a marathoner. It is the heritage of the South that God planted in my genes when He created me. It drives my husband, a natural sprinter, to exasperated distraction. I have learned to smile and wave as he passes me on the day's journey. I'll find him again by nightfall lying face down in his fatigue.

It isn't that I can't work at a fast pace. I can and I do when it is necessary. But it stresses me. And it isn't pretty. It isn't at all pretty.

Take, for example, the year I hosted a big family dinner on the Saturday evening before Easter. It was the kind of dinner a woman periodically puts together to remind her children that she can cook and declare to her husband that she can compete with his mother. I said, "No, thanks. I've got this," to all offers of help and cooked an early Easter meal for my husband, kids, nephew, nieces, and in-laws. To further impress my family, I put together a game of Jenga with giant Jenga blocks, complete with candy and prizes for the winners to be played after dinner. Nothing says "Happy Easter" like a giant bubble wand, glow-in-the-dark Mardi Gras glasses, an M&M'S coffee cup, and a battery-operated fart piano I found in the Walmart clearance aisle. To add to my hectic day of preparations, I also needed to take a chunk of time to finish shopping for the Easter bunny and attend the funeral of a dear friend's father.

When I woke up that Saturday morning, I had to set the dial on my inner metronome to its highest setting to get through the day. The needle on the dial began to shake terribly and a red light blinked a foreshadowing message "Warning! You really need to slow this sucker down!" Unfortunately, I didn't have time to stop and read the dial.

Running hard on the limited amount of sleep I had gotten Friday night, I began to cook. Before noon, I had marinated a pork loin in a soy sauce concoction, cooked my son's favorite strawberry pretzel salad, chilled six batches of Jell-O Jiggler jelly beans as requested by my daughter, made a bowl of Texas caviar, thawed blackberries for two cobblers, set out vegetables to be cooked later, cleaned the kitchen and the bathroom, and rearranged furniture to accommodate feeding a larger crowd.

Me a marathoner? Not that day! I had worked late into the previous night, gotten up almost before dawn, and sprinted through the morning. I was running at the pace of a Country Seasons Calendar Woman and a champion Virtuous Woman Wannabe.

And my brain was fried.

Because my overworked synapses had shut down as I dressed for the funeral that afternoon, I forgot it was Tater Day weekend. (For those of you who are not local to my end of Kentucky and are wondering what a Tater Day would be, put on your redneck-colored glasses and picture flea markets, funnel cakes, and a three-day traffic jam.)

Because I had forgotten it was Tater Day weekend, I did not leave home in time to work my way through the traffic and get to the funeral on time.

Because I did not get to the funeral on time, I had no opportunity to put my arms around my grieving friend.

Because I was blinded by a fog of bad-friend guilt, I missed the turnoff for Walmart and got on the highway to head home without shopping for the Easter bunny.

Because I had to go miles out of my way to turn around and go back to Walmart, I lost even more of my dinner preparation time.

Because I was counting the many ways in which I am an idiot as I walked through Walmart, I miscounted the number of children I have and did not buy enough chocolate Easter bunnies.

Because I did not buy enough chocolate Easter bunnies at Walmart, I had to make an unplanned stop at the Dollar General

Store near my house.

Because I had to stop at the Dollar General Store before I got home, I was pushing my bladder to the limits of its capacity.

Because I was pushing my bladder to its limit, I was doing a special dance through the Dollar General Store.

Because I could not continue the dance in my car, I employed the jump up and down in the seat form of bladder control as I drove home.

Because I was jumping up and down in the seat of my car on the way home, I caught sight of myself in the rearview mirror.

When I caught sight of myself in the rearview mirror, I realized that Tater Day wasn't the only thing my burned-out brain cells had forgotten as I dressed for the funeral. Although I had brushed my teeth, curled my hair and applied a coat of foundation to my face, I had stopped there. I had not put on the rest of my makeup. My face was devoid of color and appallingly lifeless except for my eyes, which held an extra sparkle because they were floating in the overflow of a brimming bladder. As I stared in horror at the reflection in the mirror, I reminded myself of what I already knew.

God did not create me to be a sprinter. Sprinting stresses me.

And it isn't pretty. It isn't at all pretty!

3 On My Knees with a Prayer and a Mop Bucket

She gives the day's work to her maidens.
Proverbs 31:15 (DBT)

Are you kidding me? The woman in Proverbs 31 has maidens? As in house maidens? As in other people to clean her house? Where is that bit of information in the list of to-dos handed out at the Virtuous Woman Wannabe Conferences?

If I had known that a VWW could have a maiden or two, events might have been different for me a few years ago when my husband gifted me with money for twelve days with a cleaning woman. Initially, I was excited about the gift. I had never had my own cleaning lady. I borrowed my sister's a couple of times, but she always made me give her lady back to her. That year, however, a cleaning woman was to be mine every first Tuesday of the month.

The first few times I returned home and found my house cleaned by someone other than myself were as thrilling as I had thought it would be. Every room of the house was clean at the same time! Because I threatened to cut off any body part that kicked off a shoe in my living room, smeared PB&J in my kitchen, or left a urine stream in my bathroom, my family kept the house clean for a couple days each month. I was able to relax in my home and bask in the glow of furniture polish applied with the grease of another woman's elbow.

However, after a few months, I learned that having a cleaning lady is harder than I thought. A little-known fact about employing another woman to clean your house is that people pleasers, like me, are compelled to clean before she comes. We pick up and put away books, toys, shoes, clothes, and other miscellaneous junk just before bedtime on the day before our cleaning ladies show up. To ensure that the kids don't get up in the night to relitter the house, we pleasers sleep on the floor outside their bedroom doors. Then we get up early the next morning to clean the bathroom before our lady arrives. We do it because even the best of cleaning women can't vacuum and dust around the clutter of five overactive kids and two drag-butt-tired parents. And because no self-respecting people pleaser I know would let another woman clean her bathroom before she cleaned it first.

Had I known then that Proverbs 31 was encouraging me to have a house maiden or two, I might have been more at ease with someone cleaning for me. But that knowledge would not have solved my other cleaning lady problem. Although I signed my name to her paycheck every month, which technically made me the woman's boss, it was difficult for me to give her direct instructions about what I needed her to do. In fact, I found it hard to give her any kind of instructions.

"What time do you want me to be at your house?" she asked when I hired her.

"Any time works for me. Why don't you pick a time that is good for you?" I hated to inconvenience her on the first day she worked for me.

"What cleaning products do you want me to use?" She was efficient and to the point.

"Whatever you prefer." I was intimidated and indecisive. I thought she would be the one to know the best cleaning products to use. "Do you need special cleaning stuff? I could run to Walmart. Can I get milk or bread for you while I am there?" I felt it was only right that I offer to run a few errands for her. She was, after all, cleaning my house for me.

"What specifically do you want me to clean?" Evidently, she had not yet realized that I had no idea what I wanted.

"Well, I've already cleaned the bathroom. You could clean the kitchen. Unless, of course, you don't do kitchens. How about the bedrooms? Can you clean the bedrooms? Maybe you could mop the floor. Or, if you don't like to mop, you could sweep instead. If that is too much trouble, you could just open the door and shoo out the dust bunnies.

"Is there anything else?" She was plainly confused at that point.

Well, of course she was. So was I. I didn't know what else to tell her. What had I missed?

"Make yourself at home. Stay as long as you like. Or feel free to leave early. There is food in the fridge. The TV remote is by the couch. Thank you so much for coming. Maybe next month maybe we can get together and clean your house."

As it turns out, not only do I have problems meeting the domestic qualifications of the woman in Proverbs 31, but I also run into trouble when the biblical instruction is to hire someone else to be domestic in my home. I am simply unable to delegate my housework to another woman. Capable or not, it seems I am destined to be my own house maiden.

Actually, I am okay with that. Not that I like housework. As Erma Bombeck said, "Housework, if done right, will kill you." But I had rather not jump, crawl, slide, or squeeze through the obstacle course of junk and clutter that is my home when I ignore my family's tendency to make a mess. Generally, I do like the place to be clean. Besides that, I have found that when my hands are busy with cleaning tasks, my brain is quiet. When my brain is quiet, my mind is more likely to find its way to the feet of Jesus.

I have found that the time I spend on the physical tasks of cleaning my house or working in my yard is likely to be a holy time with God. When my spiritual eyes open to see Him in the common places of my home, I worship. It is when I am in my kitchen working alone (except for Amy Grant, who is singing at a high volume through the speakers on the wall, and the Holy Spirit, who fills both the room and the heart within me) that I am most likely to kick off my spiritual shoes and dance before God.

Nicholas Herman was a seventeenth-century soldier who, after experiencing a life of poverty as a child and the ravages of war as a young man, found solace as a monk in a Carmelite monastery in Paris. Known there as Brother Lawrence, he was assigned to perform menial kitchen tasks because his lack of education excluded him from the more significant monastic duties. In his kitchen, Brother Lawrence found God in every cake he turned and every pot he washed. The spiritual joy and peace he found in the common business of life were so evident to the priests around him that when he died, they gathered his thoughts from his letters and notes of his interviews and compiled them into what is known as *The Practice of the Presence of God*. That little book is now considered classic Christian reading. When talking about his simple domestic tasks in the kitchen, Brother Lawrence said, "The time of business does not with me differ from the time of prayer; and in the noise and clatter of my kitchen…I possess God in as great tranquility as if I were upon my knees at the blessed sacrament."

Someday I will leave my kitchen and take my meals at heaven's banquet table. I hope to meet there many Christians with stories to tell. At some point, I would like to sit between Dietrich Bonhoeffer and Corrie Ten Boom and listen while they compare their accounts of God's faithfulness to them when they were prisoners during WWII. As I pass the potatoes to Mother Teresa, I would like to ask her what she learned of Jesus during the years she spent in the leper colonies of India. Over dessert, I would like to listen as C. S. Lewis reads aloud his favorite stories of Aslan and the grand adventures in the land of Narnia.

More than likely, it will be after the meal, when I volunteer for kitchen duty, that I meet Brother Lawrence. We'll nod in introduction. Recognizing a kindred spirit, we will smile. Then in the tranquility of worship, I'll wash and he will dry.

When the weather is warm, I much prefer working in my yard to cleaning my house. I like to be outside even when that means sweeping porches, trimming bushes, cleaning flower beds, and trampling down mole hills. Yard-work-tired is one of my favorite feelings.

At the end of those days, I drag every aching joint and muscle up the steps to our front porch and sit for a while in the swing that hangs there. With the small bit of energy I have left, I push off against the floor and set the swing into motion. As the swing rocks, I look over my yard with satisfaction in the day's work.

In those moments, when I am tired and dripping sweat in my shoes, God often sits down beside me. He brings a special kind of rest to that swing.

I begin to pray slowly. I am too hot and tired to pray quickly. "This life You gave me, it feels good."

He nods. It is good.

My heart fills with gratitude. "Thank You."

He smiles. I am welcome.

The Holy Spirit comes to join us in the breeze and whispers to me, "Look up above your own work and see what We will do."

As I raise my eyes from my yard and set them on the horizon, Jesus, creator of all things in heaven and on earth, begins to paint a sunset. The colors of compassion spread across His canvas. Mercy flows from His paintbrush and ripples over the horizon. Broad strokes of power and majesty form clouds in the sky. Sacrifice shines through and lines them with a bittersweet beauty. Peace, hope, and joy fill in the empty spaces.

And there, in the porch swing, sitting with God at the end of a work day, rest finds its way to my soul.

4 The Everlastingly Endless Question: What to Cook? What to Cook!

She gives food to her household.

Proverbs 31:15 (NASB)

As a young Virtuous Woman Wannabe, I realized that at some point it would be necessary to turn my domestic efforts to the art of cooking. One day I would need to don an apron that declared me to be a "culinary queen," raise my whisk to the sky, and reign with skill in the kingdom of my kitchen.

To date, that day has not come.

The problem with cooking is that no matter how much time and effort I put into making a meal for my family, the next day I find them sitting at the table expecting me to do it again. It is like a scene from the movie *Groundhog Day*. Every morning I awake to wonder what I will cook to eat that night. I open the door of the refrigerator-freezer and stand there in a stupor, staring at the multitude of vacuum-packed pouches, frozen bags, and prepackaged boxes crammed between the shelves and moan, "We have nothing to eat." Then I ask myself the question that will burden my thoughts for the rest of the day. "What are we going to have for supper tonight?"

Mid-morning, my plan is to serve leftovers from another meal. Then I recall that we have eaten leftovers for one or two or maybe five nights of the last week, and I realize that it would be dangerous to serve my family another meal of leftover food. For my personal safety, I would have to hide the knives and the sharp-pronged forks.

At noon I call my husband to check on his lunch plans, hoping he will leave the responsibilities of his office and meet a friend for a hearty, substantial, possibly all-you-can-eat meal. I do that because considering her husband's stress level is what a Virtuous Woman Wannabe does. If he tells me he will eat a hearty, substantial, preferably all-you-can-eat meal for lunch, I will do a little hallelujah dance and serve carrot sticks for supper. I do that because monitoring her husband's calorie intake is what a Virtuous Woman Wannabe does. If he comes home for a small lunch, I will resign myself to cooking a sizable supper and tell him I am glad to see him in the middle of the day, because sometimes little-white-lying to her husband is what this Virtuous Woman Wannabe does.

In the middle of the afternoon, I get serious about planning the meal and flip through my mental list of stock recipes. For one reason or another, I reject them all. Too many calories. Too many ingredients I don't have. Too many "yucks" from my children. Much too much trouble! Eventually, I make a decision, run to the grocery store, and cook supper for my family. The next morning, like the clock in *Groundhog Day* that clicks over to relive the same day, I find myself staring into the freezer and moaning, "We have nothing to eat!"

I have not always been this disinterested in preparing meals for my family. When I was young and idealistic, I fully intended to become a great cook. I planned to spend the Sundays of my life frying chicken in my best church dress with my sleeves rolled up so I could knead my hands in a mound of bread dough while the meringue on a chocolate pie browned in the oven behind me.

But that was then—when I didn't know. When I didn't know so many things.

I didn't know a woman has to have the forearm muscles of Popeye the Sailor to knead a loaf of bread. I didn't know making meringue requires six hands—four to handle the egg whites and two to lift toward heaven in a VWW prayer for stiff peaks. (Lord, help me! *Lord, help me now!*) I didn't know it would take two hours and a pair of long nose pliers to pull the skin off a chicken; an hour and a half to fry it; and the best part of three days to clean the grease off the top of my stove, the corners of my ceiling, the surface of my floor, and the bodice of my best church dress.

I didn't know becoming a good cook requires close attention to the task. Reading while cooking will burn the biscuits more often than not. Daydreaming will boil the water out of the beans nine times out of ten. And adding one little "b" to a recipe will ruin the dish every single time. (It is surprising what replacing a tsp. of salt with a *tbsp.* will do to a chocolate pie.)

Over the years, from necessity and perseverance, I became a decent cook. But I never enjoyed the culinary process. When my children were young, I cooked because Child Protective Services tends to show up if you starve your kids, and we couldn't afford to feed them any other way. Now I cook because a certain kind of family magic happens in the noise and chaos when my children and their families all sit down together at my kitchen table.

I suppose it is still possible that one day I will raise a whisk to the sky and become a true culinary queen in my kitchen. But I wouldn't bet the farm on it. I'm pretty sure if I waved that kitchen tool in the air, all I would get is egg in my hair. I think it is more likely I will spend the rest of my days moaning about what to cook for supper and hoping that on the day I sit down at heaven's banquet table, the meal is not potluck.

Ironically, as much as I dislike to spend time in my kitchen, I delight in the hours my family lingers at our dinner table. Gathered around that table, my husband and I have instructed, encouraged, disciplined, and laughed with our children. With my husband and I seated at either end and our children's bum cheeks scrunched together on a bench between us, that table has been our family's best school room. Sitting there over the years, our kids have learned a fork is laid on left side of a plate, math homework won't kill them, and dating is not to be taken lightly. My husband and I have taught them what we know. Most important, we have taught them what we know of God.

We aren't the only family to use the dinner table as a spiritual place of learning. I feel sure that generations of parents have done the same. Mistakes made by the first of God's people have taught us its importance.

When Moses was 120 years old, God told him he would die soon. He had spent forty years in the desert, leading the people of Israel to the land God promised them, but he would not enter it with them. Moses prepared them to complete the journey with Joshua as their leader. He wrote down all the instructions God had given to the Israelites then passed them to the temple priests. The priests were to read the instructions to the people routinely so that they would remember they belonged to God, follow the instructions God gave them, and teach their children to do the same.

> "Call them all together," the Lord instructed, "—men, women, children, and foreigners living among you— to hear the laws of God and to learn his will, so that you will reverence the Lord your God and obey his laws. Do this so that your little children who have not known these laws will hear them and learn how to revere the Lord our God as long as you live in the Promised Land." (Deuteronomy 31:12–13 TLB)

The priests of Israel took the laws of God, which Moses had given them, and carried them into the Promised Land, to be kept in the holiest place in their temple. Year after year and generation after generation, the priests read the instructions to the people whom God had chosen to be His. For centuries, the Israelites lived under the laws of God, and they faithfully taught every mark and meaning of them to their children. And yet, the written laws and commands were not enough to stir the hearts of the Israelites and remind them that they belonged to God. As the years passed, the nation of Israel repeatedly rejected God and ignored the commands He had given them through Moses.

> They abandoned Jehovah, the God loved and worshiped by their ancestors—the God who had

brought them out of Egypt. Instead, they were worshiping and bowing low before the idols of the neighboring nations…How quickly they turned away from the true faith of their ancestors, for they refused to obey God's commands. (Judges 2:12, 17 TLB)

In the 500 years after Moses, only one generation of Israelites remained faithful to God, who honored the covenant God had made with them. That was the generation of Joshua. They were the people who had first crossed into the Promised Land and had seen incredible miracles on the journey. As long as the old men who witnessed the power of God were alive to tell the stories, the children of Israel remained faithful.

The people had remained true to the Lord throughout Joshua's lifetime, and as long afterward as the old men of his generation were still living—those who had seen the mighty miracles the Lord had done for Israel. (Judges 2:7 TLB)

When God gave my husband and me children, He charged us with their spiritual training. Like the priests of the Old Testament, we have taught our children the ways and commandments of God as they are written in the Bible. We read them stories of Bible characters while they were still babies in our laps. As they grew, we taught them to study and memorize Scripture for themselves. As their parents, we desired to instill in our children a love for what is precious to us.

But there is a risk when parents teach the commandments in the

Bible to their children. In our excitement to teach them its words, in our passion to introduce them to the abundant life described in its pages, in our fervor to instruct them in the laws of God, we can overlook the fact that there is no actual power in the book. The words, in and of themselves, are just written words. It is the Holy Spirit who gives them life. As with the later generations of Israelites who heard no personal accounts of the miracles of God, Bible verses will not cause our children to seek God when they are passed to them as nothing more than words on a page.

Like the old men of Joshua's generation, those of us who want our children to know God need to also tell them our stories. Our children need to hear the ways we have experienced Him and found Him faithful. If we want our kids to spend time with God, we should talk to them about our days with Him, telling them when we see Him in the sunset or hear Him whisper in the wind. Our children need to know that, although unseen, the Spirit of God is as real to us as they are.

I first heard people telling their life stories with God in my mother-in-law's kitchen. She was a wonderful cook, and her table overflowed with the love she put into a meal. At the end of the day, over crunchy fried chicken, creamy mashed potatoes, Southern-cooked green beans that had simmered till they laid down and died in the pan, and fresh baked bread spread with butter that melted and trickled down our arms, the members of her family laughed and loved and shared with one another the events of their days. Jesus could not have been more present in those conversations if His sandals had been planted under the table with our flip flops.

In truth, I cook for three reasons: 1) avoidance of the Child Protective Services issue I mentioned earlier; 2) the joy I get from the laughter that bounces around the table when we all sit down to eat together; and 3) the knowledge that every time the supper table conversation turns to the spiritual things of life, and at our table it often does, our children are witnesses to our very real experiences with Jesus.

Like the old women of the Old Testament, as well as my mother-in-law, I will cook. I may burn the biscuits and I might read while the green beans simmer till they lay down and die, but I will cook. Then when my children and grandchildren sit down to eat at our table, my husband and I will feed them what we know of God.

By the way, the Old Testament does not record that the old women of Israel were present during the conversations about the miracles God performed in the desert. But I feel sure they were. If they had not been there, who would have corrected the details in the old men's stories?

Just sayin'.

5 Picking Peace

She considers a field and buys it;
out of her earnings she plants a vineyard.

Proverbs 31:16

I have never planted a vineyard. However, several years ago, I bought a bunch of plants with my husband's earnings and started a tomato patch. I felt like quite the Virtuous Woman that summer as I harvested my bushel baskets of tomatoes. (Actually, I picked my tomatoes and threw them into Walmart bags, but I'll never make it into a scene in a John Sloan Country Seasons Calendar if that knowledge gets around. The calendar women would never be seen with vegetable-laden plastic bags hanging from their arms. They also would never be seen crawling around their gardens on their hands and knees, dripping sweat from their belly buttons. But that is beside the point.)

As it turned out, my family could not eat bushel baskets of tomatoes no matter how hard we tried. We had tomatoes salted for breakfast, sandwiched for lunch, chopped into salads for supper, and bagged up to give to friends at church on Sundays. But still, the little buggers multiplied on my kitchen counter. It was the tomato miracle of '02, a modern-day version of the Old Testament flour and oil story. As the widow's barrel never emptied of flour and her jar never drained of oil, so my kitchen never cleared of those prolific vegetables. (Though some people claim tomatoes are fruit, tomatoes that are grown in Southern gardens and served on Southern tables are vegetables. Cooks in the South will tolerate no argument about that.)

We had tomatoes everywhere. Their juices ran over my counters, down my cabinets, and under my refrigerator, depositing tomato seeds into the dust and dirt that continually crawl under there. I worried that when watered by the broken seal on the dishwasher, the seeds would sprout a new batch of plants that would threaten my family with the tomato miracle of '03.

Knowing that a VWW would never waste a tomato, I eventually decided to freeze my surplus. The issue with freezing a tomato is that when frozen then thawed, a tomato is mushy and only good for cooked foods. That posed a problem for me. Some cooks put frozen tomatoes in soups and stews. But my husband doesn't like liquid foods because he doesn't want to eat his supper with a spoon. He believes that after a day at work slaying professional dragons, a man should come home to a hearty meal he can spear with a fork.

Other cooks might put frozen tomatoes in a homemade spaghetti sauce. But my recipe for spaghetti a la Ragu (Chunky Garden version in the 24-ounce jar) doesn't call for additional tomatoes. I believe if a no-effort meal is working, don't mess with it.

The only dish I regularly cooked for my family that would make use of my frozen harvest was my mother-in-law's recipe for breaded tomatoes. Garden tomatoes (the vegetable kind) are combined with enough butter to clog a subway tunnel and then simmered. Sugar is added to sweeten the dish until it falls just short of causing a diabetic coma. Then bread is added to sop up the juice. Anyone reared below the Mason-Dixon Line should relish this dish. It is everything Southerners love.

But with the exception of my oldest son, who still asks for breaded tomatoes on his birthday when his siblings have no say in the dinner menu, my children hated them. The year of the breaded tomato miracle was their time of determined mutiny. They knew better than to complain about the food I cooked, so they employed more subtle forms of protest. While my #1 child ate the tomatoes heartily, #2 cried a silent tear over them, hoping a respectful display of distress would gain my sympathy. Number three hid them under his napkin and hoped I wouldn't notice. While appearing compliant above the table, #4 tried to feed them to the dog underneath it. The dog refused to eat them. Number five, who was about three years old at the time, held them in her mouth for the length of the meal, trying not to touch them with her tongue, and hoped they would disappear if she didn't chew. Years later, all my children admitted to getting up from the table to make frequent trips to the bathroom, where they spit breaded tomatoes into the toilet.

That was my first and last time to plant a crop. In an attempt to earn a VWW agriculture badge, I attempted a gardening enterprise and my family suffered for it. My husband, who liked the tomatoes the first time I served them, detested them by the twenty-fifth time I set them on the table. My children, in desperate attempts to avoid eating them, resorted to emotional manipulation, canine persecution, and outright lying about the state of their bladders.

If my tomato patch gave my family that much trouble, I can

only imagine the mayhem that would have occurred if I had planted a vineyard.

Actually, I know exactly what would have happened if we had planted a vineyard. It would have been trampled under the hooves of the farm animals that officially live in our fields but routinely escape their confines to wander through our yard as if they were on a Sunday stroll.

My husband is a man with seven years of higher education who aspires to be a pretend farmer. He has a diploma hanging on his wall that allows him to practice law. Yet what he really wants to do with his time is play with animals. So ten years after we married, we bought twelve acres of land outside his hometown in western Kentucky and built the farmhouse in which we would raise our family. Over the years, my husband added a barn, put up fencing, and collected the animals that would fill our fields and officially make our acreage into a small farm. Our experiences with those animals have left my husband and me standing on opposite sides of the fence. That fence collapsed when our ram said, "Hey, Ewe, the grass is greener on the other side" and led thirty-two of his favorite girlfriends across it to trample through our yard, chew up my flower beds, and throw a slumber party in our driveway.

My husband bought our errant sheep not long after we moved to the farm because he had recently purchased a herding dog that needed something to herd. To accessorize his new hobby, he bought a long staff with a crook in the handle and carried it with him as he worked the sheep. With his dog by his side, he wandered our fields as a zealous shepherd with a short, hairy sidekick.

Our first sheep were a wooly species. They were fluffy and cute and our boys rode them bareback like cowboys in a rodeo. My husband finds that working with animals relaxes him after a stressful day at work, and the woolies were particularly entertaining to him. That is until shearing time came around. Come to find out, zealousness is a poor substitute for fleecing experience. My husband discovered that, like a day at his office, wrestling a panicked sheep with a pair of electric shears left him with a significant amount of stress. It also left him with a hideously trimmed ewe ashamed to appear naked before her friends, and a stream of his own blood flowing through his fingers.

As a result of my husband's trimming trauma, we sold the woolies and bought a species of sheep that grows hair and does not require shearing. Those animals do a dandy job of keeping our fields clear of small brush and tall grasses. They also do a pretty adequate job of dragging themselves under our fences to roam, free from captivity, through our yard. What the sheep don't understand is that many dangers are on the yard side of the fence. If they walk down the hill, stray dogs might attack them. If they cross the road, oncoming cars could run over them. And if I find them eating the flowers in my garden again, I will seriously consider hitting them between the eyes with a rake, shearing them with a rototiller, and planting their chops in my freezer.

Oblivious to the dangers, our sheep wander. They take a Sunday stroll through our yard. They meander into the road, stopping traffic with a pleading look in their eyes that begs, "Please don't tell the Mrs. where you found us." When feeling particularly adventurous, they leave our farm behind and saunter down the hill to tell the neighbors howdy.

Our neighbors would prefer that our fields grow a vineyard.

From many a point of view, our fields are a farming failure. They have never produced a Virtuous Woman's vineyard. Much of the time, they have not been able to contain the animals that live in them. There was a year, when my husband was very new at pretend farming, that their soil gave all the sheep foot rot.

However, our fields do grow blackberry bushes!

A quote by Elizabeth Barrett Browning was taped to the inside of a cabinet door in my kitchen until the paper yellowed and the sticky on the tape gave up and turned loose. For years, every time I emptied the dishwasher or got my kids a drink of water or grabbed a glass for the Diet Coke that got me through the day, I saw these words: "Earth's crammed with heaven, and every common bush afire with God, but only he who sees takes off his shoes; the rest sit round and pluck blackberries."

I assume Elizabeth Barrett Browning spent some time in her yard, pondering things of God. I do that too. As Mrs. Browning writes, earth is crammed with heaven, and God can be seen everywhere if our eyes are open to Him. In fact, for me, He can be most present in a blackberry bush. I assume Mrs. Browning would have agreed if she'd had more than one child. If she'd had a house full of children, she may have known that blackberry patches can be blessed God spots.

I have five kids who, when they were young, followed in my footsteps until they scraped the hide off my heels. They ran through the house, crying for me at the drop of every hat even if their father was in the room with them. They attached themselves to my hips like parasites and crawled into my lap for special "Mommy and me moments" every time I took a seat in the bathroom.

But those five children would not go anywhere near a thorn bramble. So for a few weeks during every June and July of their childhood, I spent early mornings alone in our blackberry patch.

I was happy to be among the brambles, wearing my oldest jeans, a long-sleeved shirt, and my husband's knee-high boots, which served to protect me from ticks, chiggers, snakes, and poison oak. My hands, which were covered with thorn scratches, looked like chipmunks had chewed them up and spit them out, but they were not digging peanut butter out of my kids' nose holes. The miniature horses in our fields licked berry juice off the seat of my pants, but my children were not wiping snot all over the front of my shirt. I was hot and sweaty but peacefully alone to be quiet and know that God is God.

Over the years, He spoke to me many times on those mornings. I didn't hear His voice with my physical ears, but the Holy Spirit put words in my thoughts that I understood. As I stood in my blackberry patch, balanced on one foot, dripping sweat in my husband's boots, bleeding from the scratches on my picking hand, and wondering if I could stretch to reach that very last berry without falling face first into the bush, a sudden breeze would rush down the hill and blow over me.

And the Holy Spirit would say, "Hey, good morning. Look! I am here!"

A vineyard? Who needs a vineyard when God meets you in the blackberry bushes?

6 I Married Peter Pan

Her husband is respected at the city gate,
where he takes his seat among the elders of the land.

Proverbs 31:23

"Let's raise a turkey for Thanksgiving this year," my husband said one spring day a few years after we bought our toy farm.

His suggestion did not surprise me. Considering the geese that attacked our children, the goat that ate the tree we planted in my mother's memory, and the pot-bellied pig that once lived in our spare bedroom, I was less than enthusiastic.

"By 'raise a turkey,' I hope you mean pick it up. And by 'pick it up,' I hope you mean drive into town and buy it at Walmart," I responded. I like my Thanksgiving turkey dressed in plastic with "Butterball" stamped across its portly chest.

"It's just a bird. How much trouble could it be?"

"That's what you said about the chickens!"

We bought chickens with the assurance that they would roost in the barn and be no problem. As it turned out, my husband and I differed on what constitutes a problem. He thought it was kind of cute when the chickens refused to stay in the barn and wandered the yard freely. I was sort of steamed when they trampled through my geraniums and scratched up my marigolds.

The traces of their presence that were left around the yard and on the porch and in the kiddie pool upset me. My husband wasn't bothered. When the rooster flogged our youngest children, it brought out every protective, motherly instinct in me. It brought out laughter in their father. I was both relieved and thankful when the Lord, evidently needing fried chicken for His banquet table, took those birds, one by one, to be with Him.

"The kids would love to raise their own Thanksgiving turkey. It would be a great learning experience for them."

With that statement, my husband played the ace he always kept up his sleeve, the reason he consistently won the animal argument. His "good for the kids" card trumped the practical defenses I had in my hand every time. So later that week, he got into his truck and drove past Walmart on his way to the county co-op where he a bought a young gobbler.

The seasons passed that year, and it seemed that my husband had been right. Our kids took on the responsibility of caring for the turkey, and we raised a fine, plump bird. Then, just before the holiday, my husband gathered us all together and proclaimed, "It's time to invite the turkey to Thanksgiving dinner."

When my husband and I were young, poor, and living in a dilapidated single-wide trailer, he often came home at the end of the day to find me brandishing a shoe in each hand, valiantly protecting our home from the cockroach population that lived in our kitchen cabinets. On those evenings, he moved me aside and stepped up to take my place at the battle station. He met the roaches eye to beady little eye and resolutely reached inside the cabinets.

I watched in horror night after night as he picked up the little vermin, gently cradling them in his hands, and then released them in the yard. By morning, they had formed a conga line with all their best buds and danced their way back into my kitchen. How was a man who would not let his wife squash a roach going to kill a turkey?

I do believe that a twenty-first-century family could successfully slaughter and prepare their own turkey in nineteenth-century style if they had an experienced person to guide them through the process. We had a newly sharpened ax and an abundance of eager ignorance.

I also believe that ignorant people like us could get the job done with a minimal amount of trouble if they had a couple of strong, hardened men assigned to the task. We had a pretend farmer who held the turkey tightly and handed the ax to his twelve-year-old son.

Maybe another boy could have killed the bird with a forceful swing. Our son turned his head and hit the bird with a timid stroke. He couldn't bring himself to look the bird in the eye and attack him with an ax.

I suppose my son's weak swing could have killed the bird if the stump my husband had laid it on had not been rotten. Instead, the decaying wood gave way and my son's blow just pushed the turkey deeper into the stump. My husband was left holding a dazed and bleeding bird as it gave him a sincere "I appreciate the offer, but I'd really rather not" to his dinner invitation.

The turkey eventually made it to our Thanksgiving table, but it was not our family's finest meal. None of us could eat him. We pushed him around on our plates as we sadly told him good-bye. Then we covered him with our mashed potatoes and gave him a proper burial.

At every junior high slumber party I ever attended, after painting our nails and before freezing the bra of the first girl to fall asleep, my friends and I made a list of the qualities we wanted in a husband. Mine were short but specific, and pretend farmer was nowhere on the list. He would be

- tall and handsome;
- preferably, dark haired, but a blond guy was acceptable if he tanned well;
- a football player because, although I understood nothing about the game, I liked the way the guys looked when they ran onto the field with their helmets under their arms and shoulder pads under their shirts (basketball players were kinda skinny and baseball players spit in the dirt);
- smart and outgoing; and
- able to play guitar and sing.

I made the list at a young age, and it didn't change much as I got older. But it wasn't quite complete. Although I never said it aloud, because I didn't have the words to understand or explain it, I also wanted a husband who would lead me into the "More" for which I often yearned, the More that called to my soul from the world around me.

My sister finds God at the beach. The Holy Spirit is very present to her as she watches the waves roll in around her feet. My husband finds Him in the woods on the back of a horse. On the day He sculpted me, God made my soul to find Him in color.

A field of wildflowers or a strikingly vivid sunset causes my heart to flip and twirl in its own little dance of spiritual worship.

When I was growing up, a tulip tree in my family's yard bloomed a vibrant pink in the spring. As I sat on our back stoop, visually contrasting the color of that tree with the deep blue of the sky, an impactful thing happened inside me. Those colors gave me a taste of something sweet to my soul, and my heart yearned for more of it. At that point, I could not identify it, but later, as a young adult, I understood that the More I desired was the presence of the Creator. Maybe I learned it from a study of Scripture, or maybe the Holy Spirit whispered it in my ear. Either way, I eventually realized my soul longed for God with the same intensity King David wrote about in Psalms. "As the deer pants for streams of water, so my soul pants for you, my God" (Ps. 42:1).

Along with all the other requirements on my husband list, I wanted to marry a man who had found the More and could lead me to it.

Two days after starting college, I met Greg Northcutt. He had a freckled complexion that didn't tan, and a large red afro that lit up like a neon sign when the sun shone through it. He wasn't particularly tall and didn't play sports of any kind. But he had great eyes, and his shoulders were strong and broad, even without the help of pads under his shirt. And the guy could make music! He could make an audience laugh or cry with the strings of his guitar and the expression in his voice. I was hooked the first time I heard him sing.

More important, Greg was God's answer to my deepest desire in a husband. He was the first person I knew who talked about Jesus as naturally as he talked about the other people in his life. For as long as I have known him, my husband has walked with God, seeking spiritual things and always looking for More.

However, although my husband passionately pursues life with God, I'm afraid he may not qualify as the husband of a Virtuous Woman. To be found sitting at the gate mentioned in Proverbs 31 and respected by the elders of the land, he would need to be an adult who doesn't mind going to meetings. My husband, although wearing the full-sized body of a man, never really grew up.

I was minding my own business. I really was.

My husband and I were at a convention in Louisville, Kentucky. As a city attorney, Greg was there to get Continuing Legal Education hours. I was there to spend time in a hotel room with nothing more important to do than sit on a bed I didn't have to make, watch a television I didn't have to dust, and throw candy wrappers into a garbage can I didn't have to empty.

Greg found me that afternoon in the hotel room writing a humor article for my blog. If I divide the amount of money I have earned writing humor by the time I have put into it, my hourly wage would begin with a decimal point. Nevertheless, it is technically income. So when Greg found me, I was in the room literally minding my own business.

He asked if I wanted to join him for lunch. I had been planning to toss three novels into a bag and walk a couple of blocks to Panera for lunch. Once there, I intended to spend a delicious hour or two in their courtyard with a bowl of butternut squash soup and whichever of the books enticed me at the moment. But Greg was wearing the look he gets when he has spent too many hours in the stressful world of adults. So I abandoned my afternoon plans and joined my husband for lunch and a few hours of playing hooky from his classes.

A friend who was also at the conference had heard a police training simulator was set up in the hotel to promote its services to Kentucky police departments. But she was pretty sure it was actually there so the convention attendees could play cops and robbers in their free time. Cops and robbers? That was exactly what Greg wanted to play after spending the morning as a professional grown-up. So we went.

I would soon face the consequences of that choice...

7 Love Covers a Multitude of Blunders

She brings him good, not harm, all the days of her life.
Proverbs 31:12

All the days? As in every single one?

Day lands!

There have been times in my life when I have wondered what God was thinking when He created men and women to be dissimilar and mismatched and then expected them to live together without harming each other. The day at the convention playing cops and robbers with my husband was one of them.

The meeting room that held the police training simulator was dark and set up like a movie theater. We watched a large screen on which a computerized program was playing dozens of variations of crime scene scenarios. The computer program was meant to be a training tool for police men and women and was available to the convention attendees as an incentive for city officials to purchase the program for their police departments. The program trainers were professional in their presentations and instructed their audience to participate in the crime scenarios thoughtfully and purposefully. Because I had not wanted to be there in the first place, I had trouble taking the situation seriously.

As I watched with one eyebrow raised in a bit of derision, men in ties and women in heels stepped up to the screen. They looked down the sights of realistic-looking toy guns to shoot virtual bad guys with pretend bullets. Having spent many of his childhood days playing cops and robbers, my husband did very well in his crime scene scenarios. Our friend Lisa also picked up a gun and shot one of the virtual men.

I sat in my chair and rooted for the two of them as they played their screen games. I figured the sooner the pretend cops eliminated the nonexistent robbers, the sooner I could go and introduce myself to the characters who were waiting for me in my books. Although those characters also lived in imaginary worlds, I was pretty sure their settings would be more rational than the one I was in at the moment. I had just watched a lady giggle as she shot through the private parts of a man who wasn't really in the room.

When Greg and Lisa completed their crime scenarios and I thought we were finally ready to leave, Greg looked at me and said, "I think you should try this. What do you think?"

What did I think?

I thought *no way* was I going to try that! I had never held a handgun. I'm a lousy shot with a rifle. And I had left my policewoman uniform hanging in the closet at home with my Batgirl mask and my Wonder Woman push-up bra.

Nevertheless, a few minutes later, I was standing at the front of the room with a gun in my hand. I had learned to use the sights on the gun to aim it, and I had hit the practice targets with only one miss. Evidently, I was not a lousy shot.

I had already shot a guy with terrible hygiene habits and a gun hidden under his jacket. Granted, I had previously seen his scenario so I already knew he was a bad guy, but I hit him dead in the heart. I thought that was pretty impressive. I was ready to holster the gun and walk off into the sunset. Just beyond the view of the sunset from the lobby windows were the elevators to the upstairs rooms and the books that awaited me.

But the man running the simulator program suggested I run through one more scenario, so I aimed the gun at the screen again. When the next video began, I found myself looking at the door of a virtual bedroom. The instructor had told me that in this scenario I was in my own home. My husband and I had been awakened by a noise, and he had gone to investigate, leaving me in the bedroom with the gun.

At that point, the storyline had already veered from the realm of my personal probability because on the few times in our marriage that Greg has gotten up to investigate a suspicious noise, I have given him a thumbs-up for good luck, turned over, and gone back to sleep. I'm not much of a worrier.

Wanting to do well in this simulation, I knew from watching the other scenarios that anything could happen at any time. I told myself to pay attention to the doorway. But I kept getting distracted by the things in the room.

Keep an eye on the bedroom door.

What an odd color for a bedroom door. When was the last time the carpet was vacuumed over there by the bedroom door? Just look at how much dust is on the book lying by the bedroom door. Oh, I love that book!

Don't get distracted!

Keep your eyes on the doorway. Don't look at anything other than the doorway. Don't look at anything in the room. Don't look at the antique dresser in the room. Oh, I think my grandmother had an antique dresser like the one in the room!

Pay attention!

Do I see anything? I see lots of things. I see that there is mail on the nightstand. Who gets mail in a pretend crime scene scenario? Maybe it's my mail. No, it can't be my mail. Can I read the address on the mail? No, I'm too far away to read the address on the mail. Maybe the guy by the door can read the address on the mail.

The guy by the door!

Suddenly, there he was…the guy in my crime scene scenario. My job was to assess whether or not he posed a threat to me and shoot him if he did.

Was he a threat? I wasn't sure. I didn't know the guy. But, realistically, how would we have ever met? I live in the real world and he lives in a stream of light projected on a wall.

He was in my pretend house without being invited. That was true. But I didn't know why he was there. Perhaps his pretend car had broken down and he wanted to use our pretend phone. And when our pretend doorbell had not worked, he picked our pretend lock and came looking for help.

Did he intend to hurt me? Well, that was hard to say. He held a knife in his hand, but I didn't know why. Perhaps while walking through the house he had noticed a mess in the kitchen and stopped to do a few of the dishes. If that was the case, I needed to thank him. I didn't know what my pretend husband was doing at the moment, but I was pretty sure he wouldn't stop to clean anything.

The guy glistened with sweat. Clearly agitated, he had a wild, rabid look in his eyes. Well, there was my answer. There was no threat there. The poor guy was obviously sick. What could I do to help him? Somebody needed to run to the store to get this guy some medicine. Where was that pretend husband when I needed him?

Before I could do anything to help, the guy in my scenario turned and ran away. I thought he was probably going home, where his mother could take care of him.

That was not what my real husband thought. He thought I was a fool for letting an intruder run free in the house. I could hear him saying so behind me. I turned to face Greg, and the look on his face indicated what he was about to do. He was going to attack my sanity! I knew exactly how he would do it. He would pick up a few "What were you thinking?" comments, soak them in a "That's the dumbest thing I've ever seen!" tone of voice, and throw them at me.

Well, if he wanted me to react differently to a threat, I would react differently. I turned around, took a breath, and steadied my nerves. My job was to assess whether or not my husband posed a threat to me and stop him if he did.

Did I perceive a threat? Yes, I did.

Was I prepared to deal with it? Yes, I was.

With his first scoffing remark, I raised my arm, took aim down the sights of the gun in my hand, and took a shot at my husband and his sarcastic remarks.

In addition to wishing my husband a minor amount of harm, I have occasionally broken a few other rules of a VWW's polite society. I once went five years without going to the dentist. I have been known to smuggle Coke bottles and candy packages into a movie theater in my purse. And the scissors I accidentally took from my daughter's school room, the ones labeled PROPERTY OF THE KINDERGARTEN CLASS, I didn't return them!

If those things surprise you, you will be astounded to learn that when my youngest child was a baby, a warrant was issued for my arrest by a district court in Kentucky. I blame that blunder on my husband.

This is the story of my legal misconduct.

The Crime: A city police officer pulled me over for driving fifteen miles over the speed limit.

The Appeal: I stuffed the box of dry cereal I had been eating for breakfast under the seat and wiped my mouth with our infant daughter's spit-up rag. (It was the only faux napkin available other than the used tissue on the floor and the ketchup-covered Burger King bag in the back seat.) Then I appealed for leniency with the best smile and slight eyebrow flirt I could muster after twenty years of marriage.

The Denial: Evidently, the police officer was not impressed with my grinning grimace or with the odor of Honey Nut Cheerios and dried baby puke on my breath, because he handed me a ticket and a three-figure fine.

What My Lawyer Said: My husband, the lawyer, said a lot of things that I won't repeat, but his last words were, "Don't pay the fine. I'll take care of it." A few weeks later, a warrant was issued for my arrest for failure to appear in court to pay that fine. My lawyer had not taken care of it.

My Response: I did not consider suing my lawyer because that would come back to bite me in the bank account. However, Virtuous Woman Wannabe or not, I did not bring my husband anything good that day. In fact, I threw a few "What were you thinking?" comments soaked in my own "That's the dumbest thing you've ever done!" tone of voice.

I was upset with my husband for quite a while. But then I began to see possibilities in the situation. I wondered what would happen if I welcomed the arresting deputy into my home, took the warrant from his hands, and willingly went to jail? I would either have a little quiet time to myself or have the opportunity to make some interesting, new friends. Of course, I would have to insist that the deputy stay and take care of my kids, but he had agreed to hazardous duty when he pinned on his badge.

After a few urgent phone calls, my husband got the warrant dismissed. I admit to being a bit disappointed when that happened. A part of me was looking forward to an encounter with the police. I had thought about the situation carefully and decided I would not remain silent.

"Hello, deputy. I'm willing to go to the police station, but you need to stay here with my children. Load all the kids into my car and take #1 out for practice driving time. Make #2 do her bathroom chores. Stick your head in the toilet bowl to make sure she cleaned under the rim. Number 3 has a model of the solar system due tomorrow. Do not, under any circumstances, let him help with the project, but make it look like fourth grade work. Make two dozen clown-face cupcakes for #4 to take to school in the morning. And #5 has been sitting in a wet diaper so long her bum cheeks have shriveled up like raisins You should do something about that.

"I need to borrow the keys to the squad car so I can drive myself to jail. Insist that I go directly to jail. Do not let me pass Walmart. Do not let me stop and collect groceries. You are on duty until my husband gets home. When he arrives, feel free to leave him with the children, unarmed and outnumbered. While he is serving here in harm's way, I will be running the siren on the squad car in a boisterous accompaniment to the 'Hallelujah Chorus' I'll be singing while I'm gone."

My husband and I have experienced more than our fair share of marital blunders. But, as Peter Pan tells Wendy, "To live will be an awfully big adventure."

For the two of us together, it certainly has been.

8 In the World but Often Not Paying Attention to It

She keeps a close eye on the conduct of her family.
Proverbs 31:27 (GW)

I received the letter in the middle of December a few years ago. *The middle of December!* What government bureaucrat thought it would be a good idea to send an important document to a woman who is low on sleep, high on stress, and strung out on Christmas sugar? I am sure it was a man. A man who did not have to duplicate his dead mother's recipe for cornbread dressing, find a pair of canine antlers so the family dog could pass for a reindeer, or shop at Walmart on the Saturday before Christmas.

I skimmed the letter and put it aside. I had other, more important things to read. My husband needed me to research the mechanical specifications for the Celestron AstroMaster 90AZ Refractor Telescope we were considering as a Christmas gift. My son needed me to proofread a composition he had written for graduate level study at his seminary. My grandchildren needed to know about the holiday drama on its way to Llama Llama. The legal summons to report for jury duty in our District Court of the Kentucky Judicial System would just have to wait.

In retrospect, I should have read the thing.

The second week of January, my summons and I reported, just

a wee bit late, to the local courthouse. When I walked into the courtroom, the clerk was already giving instructions to the on-time jurors. I heard, "Let me say one more time, if any of you failed to mail in your juror questionnaire, please give it to me now."

Juror questionnaire? What juror questionnaire? I glanced at the summons and read, for the first time, the papers attached to it. There it was in big black letters: "Juror Questionnaire. Complete and return within five days of receipt."

My mind whirled. How was I going to get that thing completed and delivered to the woman at the front of courtroom without looking like an idiot? How was I going to get it done in the forty-five seconds before the judge took his place at the bench?

I slid onto the back row of seats and frantically filled out the questionnaire that I was supposed to have mailed to the clerk a month earlier. I signed my name, dotted one i, crossed two ts, smudged the date to make it illegible, and was done before the man in the robe walked in!

I surreptitiously handed the form to the clerk and returned to my seat as the judge entered and began talking to the potential jury members. My mind calmed and I began to think again. I began to think about the form I had just completed and realized that I couldn't remember many of the questions or any of my answers. Evidently, I had been in such a hurry, I filled it out without engaging the part of my brain that controls intelligent thought.

I was pretty sure I had written my name correctly. Same for my address. Had the form asked for my age? Did I give it to them or did I say, "None of your big, fat business"?

When it asked for a spouse's name, which of my husband's

names had I put on the form? Did I call him Gregory, Greg, Kaybee (a name I sometimes call him in fun), or Jerkface (a name I sometimes call him in my head or under my breath)?

Am I a US citizen? Had I checked yes, or no? Do I have mental problems? Well, of course, I do. My life is overflowing with crazy. But had I admitted that to a man with the power to declare me incompetent?

And did I recall a question about vomiting up celery? That wasn't right.

Comets named Melanie? No.

Committing a felony? That was the question! Had I told the Kentucky Court System I had committed a felony?

When the clerk read my questionnaire, would the man with the badge take me away? Would I be put on a secret government watchlist for crazies? Would someone tell my husband that he had married an airhead, or that I think his name is Jerkface Northcutt?

My husband already knows he married an airhead. If he had heard about my trouble with the questionnaire that morning, he would have told me it could have been avoided. He would have said it was caused by my inattention.

Personally, I think the fault lies with the male bureaucrat.

I would like to say I keep a close eye on the conduct of my family, but the truth is that it is hard for me to keep a close eye on much of anything. Paying attention to the world around me has been a problem all my life. The default setting on my brain takes me to a place where absentmindedness is the norm. To date, I have not been able to adjust the setting. I have found no mind-altering drugs, no mental toothpicks for propping open the eyes of my mind, no way to superglue the bum cheeks of my brain to a chair to keep my thoughts from wandering off.

The tendency to be inattentive has caused me all kinds of problems. I have been late to most of my life's appointments because I am apt to daydream while I drive, which causes me to pass my destination a time or two or five. I once Clairol-colored a red streak down my dark brown hair because I wasn't paying attention and bought the wrong box of root dye for my hair. I showed up so often at my kids' elementary school with permission slips I forgot to sign or lunches I forgot to make that the office staff thought I worked there and left me in charge of the phones while they went to lunch.

Worse than that were the times I failed to pick up my kids from school and left them waiting for me. My children learned to be good waiters because, although my husband and I differ in almost every other way, we both had a tendency to leave our kids places when they were young. By "leave them," I mean we took them out with us and forgot to bring them home again. By "places," I mean anywhere and everywhere locally, certain regions of western Kentucky, and as far east as Gatlinburg, Tennessee.

It happened so often, I labeled the leavings to keep them straight in my mind. "The Youngest" incident happened when our fourth child was eighteen months old. After visiting in the home of family friends, we told our three oldest children to get into the car, but we forgot to load the littlest one. Fifteen miles down the road, I turned around and found an empty car seat. After we left, our friends turned around and found our toddler.

"The Dumbest" leaving occurred when son #3 wanted to go to basketball practice with son #2 so he could watch the older boys play ball. I took two boys to the school gym and dropped them off. Two hours later, I drove back to the gym, picked up the older boy and left the younger one there.

We left a daughter at the library once. I consider that occasion to be "The Acceptable One". She was there with nothing to do but read and with none of us there to distract her. How could that be bad?

"The Bad Incident" happened when we left church one Sunday, drove to McDonald's for lunch, lined up our kids to ask them what they wanted to eat, and noticed we were missing one.

It is true that each time my husband and I left our kids, we eventually returned to pick them up. I gave birth to five children, and five children are in our latest family photo. I'm pretty sure they are the same five. None of them show signs of emotional trauma, so I don't think we inflicted any long-term, parental harm.

Nevertheless, there were several years when I wondered if so many children should be in my physical, emotional, and spiritual care. Even if I knew where the five of them were, would I remember to feed them all? Would I think to teach each of them to tie their shoes and wash their hands before they left the bathroom? Could my husband and I train up the whole bunch in the ways they should go to become confident, productive adults or to find their individual ways to God?

"Train up a child in the way he should go, even when he is old he will not depart from it." That is Proverbs 22:6 from The New American Standard Version of the Bible. The New Living Translation says, "Direct your children onto the right path, and when they are older, they will not leave it."

Much of Christian parenting hangs from this verse. If we, as Christian parents, teach our children the principles of God, they will follow them when they are adults.

I'm pretty sure it is not that simple.

Some Bible scholars think that in the original Hebrew language, Proverbs 22:6 reads more like The International Standard Version, which says, "Train a child in the way appropriate for him, and when he becomes older, he will not turn from it."

This interpretation suggests that children are more likely to continue in the principles of their training when they are taught according to the aspects of their personality bents. When teaching children, we parents would be wise to consider the things that make our children feel loved and the things that hurt them, to think about their creative strengths and their moral weaknesses, to keep in mind the individual traits that God gave them when He sat down with his tongue between his teeth and created their souls.

On the subject of training up children, it seems that the writer of Proverbs advises parents to know their kids. He would, no doubt, tell us to observe their ways. More than likely, he would suggest that we listen when they talk. I'll bet he would also expect eye contact on our part. If we have five children, he would probably advise that we know every one of them.

Day lands!

In my experience, training children to walk with God, like

training them to do anything else, is not simple. It is complicated and messy. (I have three sons and two daughters. Keeping their training specific to each of their personalities was complicated. The chocolate that kept me sane while the five of them talked to me tended to be messy.)

However, as a young mother, I could manage complicated and messy. It was the responsibility of training my children in spiritual things that overwhelmed me. When I was stumbling all over my own path to God, how would I ever direct the five of them onto theirs?

In keeping with Murphy's law, when my husband goes out of town, something on our little farm goes wrong. Fairly often, it is our children. When our oldest son was a teenager, my husband left for a week. After seven days of dealing with family and farm life alone, I was teetering on the brink of emotional implosion. On Sunday morning, my oldest son looked me in the eye, disrespected with abandon, and pushed me over the edge. After several minutes in my son's room asking a series of lengthy and loud questions about the idiocy that was rolling around in his head, I returned to my bedroom and threw out a few more questions at God.

"Lord, what was he thinking? Lord, what am going to do about it? How am I ever going to make him into an adult who is reasonable and useful to You?" My words were a way to blow off steam as much as they were a prayer. But God heard them and surprised me with a response. While I stood at my closet door, He spoke within my thoughts.

"Child! Let Me make this clear to you. I am the One who will be making your son into an adult. I will draw him down the path that will lead him to Me. I will grow him to be useful. You can calm down and leave it in My hands."

Philippians 1:6 says that God will perfect the work He started in those He has redeemed. Years earlier, I had found that verse and my mind already believed God would work in my children. But when the Holy Spirit spoke that fact directly to my soul, it made a spiritual rather than mental impression. My mind can become confused and doubt God. But when the Holy Spirit speaks something, my soul tends to rest in it without wavering.

I train my children according to the instructions I find in the Bible and do my best to teach them according to their own personality bents. But I do it because God has instructed His people to teach their children about His ways not because the Bible guarantees that if I do so my children will not depart from them. The book of Proverbs is a compilation of truisms. They are not promises from God. Teaching our children about God doesn't guarantee that they will choose a life with Him.

When I need reassurance about the paths my children will take, I remember what God told me about my son that day. Year after year, child after child, stupid parenting mistake after stupid parenting mistake, I replayed those words in my head and they always gave me peace.

I can live with the multitudes of parenting mistakes I make because God is keeping a close eye on the conduct of my family.

9 Family Circuses and Wild Goose Chases

Her children will rise up and call her blessed.
Proverbs 31:28 (ESV)

When my children were young, I cut a *Family Circus* cartoon out of the Sunday paper. In the cartoon, Mommy walks into Billy's room to find toys, clothes, and a variety of sporting equipment covering his floor. An overflowing trash can, a metal fire truck, a broken snare drum, and a big blue dinosaur are fighting for space on his bed. His dresser is covered with books. The pictures on the wall are askew. Underwear is hanging on the rim of a lamp shade.

In a moment of frustration, Mommy yells, "Billy, I wish you would grow up!" In the next segment of the cartoon, a picture of an adult Billy packing his car to leave home flashes into Mommy's thought bubble, and she pulls her still small son into her arms and says, "But not too soon."

A yellowed copy of that cartoon is hanging on my refrigerator door, and I have looked at it every day for the past twenty-five years. On some days, it was the reasoning that kept me from pinching off the heads of my children, convincing me I might miss them if they were gone. On most days, it was a reminder to enjoy my children while they were still home with me.

My husband and I always wanted a big family and gave ourselves to the act of parenting when our children were born. As they grew in size and number, we realized that to conserve our time, energy, and mental stability, we would need to become organized in our efforts. So we divided the parental duties between us according to our strengths and weaknesses. I took charge of teaching manners, grammar, personal hygiene, respect, work ethics, and all aspects of responsibility. Greg oversaw the facets of our children's training that best suited him: music, animal care, tree house building, toy purchasing, and a general respect for nonconformity. He also taught them to laugh…often and with gusto.

Although we divided our time and abilities when teaching our children, Greg and I came together in our philosophy about safeguarding them from the world. I like to think we had a relaxed, untroubled approach. Social services might have called it apathetic. Or they might have called it irresponsible with a fair-to-middlin' amount of negligence thrown in on bad days.

We let our children climb trees, crash vehicles, and hit one another with a variety of makeshift weapons. One of our kids fell flat on his back from the steps of a treehouse. Another hurtled into a tree while riding a zipline through our yard. A third drove the go-cart into the swimming pool.

Our children also faced a few dangers from the animals that roamed our yard. Our youngest daughter, who routinely rode horses with her daddy while he pretended to be a cowboy, was stepped on by his stallion. Our youngest son, who had egg gathering duty during the years we had chickens, was regularly flogged by our rooster. And the most extreme instance of abuse-by-animal happened when one of our geese attacked our oldest son.

You may not know that geese can be aggressive. Our birds shed aggression as young goslings and replaced it with new growths of hatefulness. Soon after that, they molted into a state of downright meanness. They stalked our yard like soldiers eager for battle, watching for the first person to abandon the safety of the porch. When they spied a potential victim, they lowered their heads and charged with a cry intended to both proclaim war and petrify the enemy. While we owned those birds, only the hardiest of our friends continued to visit. The effort required to sprint from their cars to our porch in order to avoid the incoming geese was too much for the ill, the elderly, and the faint of heart.

The skirmish between the goose and our nine-year-old son, Ben, happened while he was on a mission to the garage. He had made a strategic error letting the goose come between him and the house. Seeing the bird approaching with malice in its eyes, Ben began to slowly walk backward, his hands raised in surrender. The goose met him, eye to terrified eye, and prepared to attack. Ben, beginning to panic, sped up his retreat. His attempted flight caused the bird to advance quickly and assault the poor boy in a very personal way. As I watched in horror and my husband guffawed from the front porch, our screaming son ran backward through the yard with a goose attached to his little boy parts.

With each accident and animal incident, Greg and I addressed the tears. We applied Band-Aids, kissed boo-boos, talked about the rules of safety and animal husbandry, and tried to protect our children from the dangers that could seriously hurt them. But we didn't shield our kids from all the perils that childhood brought to them. We figured that every time they fell down, they learned a little about getting back up.

In *The Voyage of the* Dawn Treader, the third book in The Chronicles of Narnia series, C. S. Lewis writes an allegorical fantasy about three children who are magically drawn into a painting hanging on their bedroom wall of a Narnian sailing ship. After being pulled aboard the ship, the *Dawn Treader*, they join King Caspian of Narnia in a quest to search for seven missing lords. It is on this voyage that the children, Lucy and Edmund Pevensie and their bad-tempered cousin, Eustace Scrubb, sail to the eastern end of the world.

As the adventures on the *Dawn Treader* unfold, the Narnian lion character, Aslan, appears periodically to give help to the voyagers, to turn them away from danger, and to encourage them along the journey. In *The Lion, the Witch and the Wardrobe*, the first book in The Chronicles Of Narnia, it is obvious that Aslan is an allegorical picture of Jesus. Lewis also makes this plain near the end of this book when he writes that in our world, Aslan is known by another name.

Realizing that Aslan is a picture of Jesus gives allegorical meaning to the adventures that take place on the *Dawn Treader*. When Eustace Scrubb, whom Lewis describes as a boy who almost deserves his name, is changed by greed and selfishness into a dragon, he tries in vain to scrape the terrible dragon scales from his skin. Aslan comes to him and says, "You will have to let me undress you." Aslan peels the dragon skin from Eustace, throws the boy into a pool of water, and dresses him in new clothes, which surely symbolize the salvation, baptism, and new creation works of Jesus. When Edmund and King Caspian are blinded by the lure of gold and when Lucy is deceived by the enticements of physical beauty, Aslan appears to direct them away from temptation. And in a beautiful portrayal of comfort, when the *Dawn Treader* enters into a place of darkness, the voice of Aslan is heard.

In those moments, the world becomes black. No one onboard the ship can see even a glimmer of light. There is a cry of terror in the air. The hands on the tiller are shaking, frightened by what is real and unreal. When they all fear they will never escape the darkness, Lucy leans over the rail and whispers, "Aslan, Aslan, if ever you loved us at all, send us help now." A light appears and an albatross circles the mast of the *Dawn Treader*, calling out in a strong, sweet voice as it spreads its wings and rises to guide the ship into the light. As the albatross circles, Lucy feels a delicious breath on her face and hears the voice of Aslan whisper, "Courage, dear heart."

Like the characters on the *Dawn Treader*, darkness will come to my children. As their mother, I try not to pray it away. What I want most for them is to see and hear what Lucy experienced. I want them to look up for guidance, to hear the strong, sweet voice of the Holy Spirit, and to feel the delicious breath of God on their faces. I have found those things are experienced most poignantly in fear and suffering.

Pain tends to focus our attention on God. Although it hurts me to see my children in physical or emotional pain, sometimes God puts suffering on the path that leads to spiritual dependence on Him. So I don't pray a hedge of protection around my children. If it takes an illness or the loss of a job to cause my sons to look up for guidance, I don't want them to be hidden from those hardships.

Although I tell my children that there are dangers in the world and I teach them not to make sinful choices in life, I don't pray that God will keep them safe from worldly temptations. The consequences of sin and disobedience can knock us facedown at the feet of Jesus. If an unplanned pregnancy was to be the circumstance that would cause my daughter to raise her face to God and feel his breath on her cheek, I would not want to pray sexual purity for her.

My greatest desire for my children is that they know and love God deeply. So my prayer for them is "Lord, draw them to yourself." Because God created my children, He knows their strengths and their weaknesses. He knows which of life's storms will destroy them, which they can weather, and which will bring them running to Him. I leave the charting of their paths to Him. If suffering is what God uses to draw my children to Himself, I take a deep breath, pray for strength and wisdom, and trust that He knows what He is doing.

When pain comes to our children and life knocks them to their knees, Greg and I encourage them to look up and listen. Although we tell them what we know of God, it is when they hear the voice of the Holy Spirit for themselves that they learn it is strong and sweet. We trust that in the darkness, when they cry out for help and God whispers to them, "Courage, dear heart," the Holy Spirit will tuck our children under His wings and they will rise up.

Our children are no longer at home with Greg and me. I helped each of the five gather their possessions from the floor of their closets and the corners of their rooms and the far reaches under their beds. We washed the dirty underwear we found in suitcases and rain boots and old gym bags. We packed their clothes, stored their treasures in the attic, and loaded their cars with the stuff they would take to their new homes. Then I watched as my children drove off to grown-up lives. I thought of the cartoon hanging on my refrigerator door and I prayed, "It's too soon, Lord. It is much too soon!"

My children found jobs and scattered as they moved away. Three of them have married and added in-laws to the family. My oldest has his own kids to love and train. Periodically, I encourage him not to pinch the heads off his children because I know for certain he would miss his kids if they were gone.

Do my children now rise up and call me blessed? I don't know. Frankly, I'm happy if they just think to rise up and call me.

10 Fit as a Squeaky Fiddle; Strong as an Arthritic Ox

She dresses herself with strength
and makes her arms strong.

Proverbs 31:17 (ESV)

I start a diet every January. It is, after all, the official period for weight loss among American women. Evidently, some think-tank guys graduated at the bottom half of their think-tank classes and didn't qualify to think about the tanking economy, world hunger, or nuclear disarmament. Instead, they thought about the month of January and decided to declare it National Diet Month.

Since this is the same January that follows November's Thanksgiving holiday and December's Christmas season, I think it is an appropriate designation. However, I don't need a calendar to tell me it is time to end the two-month Gala of Gluttony, clean the feast out of my fridge, and stop eating puppy chow mix for breakfast. (Since the two major ingredients in puppy chow are Crispix and powdered sugar, I figure it is basically a sugared cereal and, therefore, a perfectly legitimate breakfast food.) The fit of my jeans does a fine job of communicating that message.

Although I have good intentions, I procrastinate during the first week of each January and don't do anything to lose weight other than sleep through breakfast on New Year's Day. I usually don't procrastinate during the second week of January. I just wait a few more days before seriously trying to slim down. Around the third or fourth week of the month, I get serious about making healthy changes in my lifestyle. Most years, I join an online fitness program, exercise regularly, count a few calories, and gain up to five pounds.

That has caused me to ponder the validity of National Diet Month. With some research, I discovered that January is also National Bath Month and National Dried Plum Breakfast Month, which I believe is just a more appealing name for National Prune Month. So it seems that January just doesn't have the muscle to motivate me.

A little more research told me the month of February is Wise Health Consumer Month, Return Shopping Carts to the Supermarket Month, and National Boost Your Self-Esteem Month. So when January fails to implement my weight loss plan, I look to February, hoping that month will teach me to consume smarter snacks, get a little exercise at the grocery store, and boost a few things. Self-esteem isn't really at the top of my list, but I'll take what I can get.

In March or April of each year, I begin to burn some calories by walking a few miles a week in a park near my home. On those first days of exercise, I may experience leg cramps, knee pain, heart palpitations, and asthmatic respiratory distress, but the worst of the agony is not a product of physical pain. It is caused by the potential for unbecoming psychological embarrassment.

Although many women are well-groomed when they exercise, I am not one of them. Although many women are well-dressed when they exercise, I am not one of them either. I am the woman who is unwashed, uncombed, and unadorned with the makeup that prepares her for public viewing. I am the woman who is clothed in her most comfortable clothes—tattered pants and a threadbare shirt I bought from a throwback beatnik artist on a beach in Key West, Florida, in 1991.

By the time the summer months roll around, I am serious about an exercise regimen and am walking four miles a day in my unkempt state. Occasionally, I meet the well-groomed, well-dressed women on the park trails and suffer the agony of embarrassment. If I know the women, I casually bend down to tie a shoe so they can't see my face and realize the mess in walking shoes is me. If I meet a woman I do not know, I smile and nod, keeping my hands in my pockets lest she think I am a vagrant and try to drop a dollar or two in my palm. The women have never mentioned my bedraggled appearance, but a kind-hearted teenager, apparently thinking I was in need of help, once approached with concern and asked if I knew Jesus.

Actually, on most days, I have Jesus there with me, enjoying the colors of the park and talking about things while we walk. Often, we step together to the rhythm of Amy Grant's music in my earbuds. While Amy sings her praise to the Lord, I power walk, gasping for breath as I go. Periodically, I will raise my hands and wave them in the air both as an act of silent praise and a visual plea to God for the extra strength I need to get my tired bum up the big hills. At those points in my walk, I'm sure the well-groomed, well-dressed women think I am a wackadoodle vagrant. Regardless of what others may think, I am not lifting my hands to signal my insanity. I am thoughtfully singing songs of worship with my invisible friends, Amy and Jesus.

In the fall, as the temperatures drop and the daylight hours decline, I begin to experience sluggishness and general lethargy. I have researched my symptoms on the Internet, and it seems that I have Seasonal Affective Disorder (SAD), a chronic condition brought on by a lack of sunlight, which makes me feel…well… sad. Apparently, SAD is a life-threatening disease because every year it causes me to threaten the lives of my husband, my children, and every other person I know who spent the wonderfully long, warm days of summer praying for the onset of autumn.

The symptoms of SAD are boredom, depression, lethargy, and muddled thinking. Muddled thinking! Now there's some good news. It reassures me that I am not losing my mind when I can't remember what I was going to say or why I entered a room or where I put my children. I am just SADly confused. Unfortunately, studies have found that people with SAD tend to crave sweets. Of course, I already knew that. Every woman alive has known since entering puberty that the natural treatment for problems related to lethargy and depression is chocolate.

Due to SAD, I spend the fall of every year too lethargic to exercise and self-medicating with sugar. Autumn baking is the opening ceremony for the Gala of Gluttony I will celebrate over the Thanksgiving holiday and Christmas season. And so, every December finds me stocking a feast in my fridge, eating puppy chow for breakfast, and regaining the weight I may have lost during the year.

Then, in January, I start a diet.

The Proverbs 31 Woman dresses herself with strength and makes her arms strong. I dress myself in sweats and hold my arms to my side to keep them from jiggling. Although I still want to be an example of a virtuously fit woman, I'm afraid that train has left the station. Age and motherhood have taken a toll on my body. I gave birth to five children, nursed them through infancy, consumed large amounts of chocolate to get me through their childhood years, and aged quickly when they entered adolescence and adulthood. At this point in my life, I have lost the physical strength and fitness of my youth.

Unfortunately, I have also lost the mental strength and fitness of my younger years. I recognized this for the first time several years ago when I was leaving Walmart with my youngest daughter and a buggy loaded with food and supplies for her twelfth birthday party. I turned to tell her to stay close to me in the parking lot, and with a flash of clarity, I saw a budding young lady where my baby had been.

It was then I realized that time had taken off, flown by, and gone on to circumnavigate the globe a couple of times while I wasn't looking. I stopped at the sliding door to let Tessa walk out first. I didn't want her to see the tears in my eyes. I also did not want her to realize that as time soared by, I got caught in the turbulence, and it left me addlepated and unable to remember things. Things like where the crap I had parked the car that day. My plan was to covertly follow my daughter's memory to the minivan and hope mine could find the way home.

As we pulled out of the parking lot, I began a prayer vigil for my daughters that I have continued over the years. I have prayed the Lord will circle his angels around them and keep them safe. I will need them to care for me as time picks up speed and mental deterioration rushes my way. I will need them to

- stand beside me in public and whisper in my ears the names of acquaintances in town, friends from church, and those of my family who don't call regularly;
- recover my lost items: my purse, my shoes, my Diet Coke bottle, and the Fisher Price keys my family will have given me when they take away the set that actually starts the car;
- follow me throughout the day, turning off stove burners, blowing out kitchen fires, and closing the flaps of my robe as I wander the neighborhood; and
- prepare me for wandering the neighborhood by matching my house shoes to my robe and licking their fingers to blend in the blush I will have applied to my forehead.

It is important for me to have safeguards in place. Because time is beginning to stall, and I may soon find myself crash-landing into the Sea of Senility.

Because my hands and arms are not fit and strong, I have trouble opening jar lids. I spend a good ten minutes gritting my teeth and trying to pop the lid off a jar. Then I hold the jar between my legs and twist to add the torque of my rotating shoulders. I scream with the hope that a high pitch will vibrate the lid loose. I hit it one or two times with the handle of a knife to release the vacuum that has built up in the jar. Then I hit it one or fifteen times with the head of a hammer to release the stress that has built up in me. After my attempts and failures, my husband rolls his eyes at my frailty and opens the jar with a quick twist of his wrist. He acts as if it is no big deal. But I can tell he enjoys the deed.

Because my mental vigor has been diminished by the early onset of I-can't-remember-anything-and-by-anything-I-mean-*everything*, I need my children to fill in my memory blanks. Where did I lay my cell phone? When did I last have my car keys? What did I say we were having for supper? Why did I put bug repellant in the dishwasher? They shake their heads and roll their eyes with derision as only a parent's own children can do. But it seems to me they get an inordinate amount of pleasure from filling in my blanks.

For one reason or another, my family likes me to need them. Although I would prefer to bring the strength of a Virtuous Woman into our group dynamic, giving them a peek at my weakness is a good thing. When my husband opens the jar that will become the Ragu to my spaghetti, a little moment passes between us in which he and I both know I need him. When my children realize I have lost my bright red minivan in the parking lot, they link their arms through mine and we walk together to find my car. Like it or not, weakness forces me to step closer to my family.

It also drives me to God, who, best I can tell, doesn't roll His eyes at my lack of strength. In fact, I think He is glad to see it.

The apostle Paul is considered to be one of the world's most influential Christians. He spread the gospel throughout the Roman Empire, founded many of the earliest gentile churches, and wrote a good portion of the New Testament. Along with obvious leadership skills and strong personality traits, Paul was given a weakness. He called it a thorn in his flesh and begged God to take it from him. In a letter to the church in Corinth, Paul wrote that God did not remove the thorn. Instead, God told him, "My grace is all you need. My power works best in weakness." Paul then went on to claim, "So now I am glad to boast about my weaknesses, so that the power of Christ can work through me" (2 Cor. 12:9 NLT).

I cannot honestly say I boast about my weaknesses. (I usually will do my best to open the jar lid by myself and, more often than not, will wind my way in and out of parked cars, looking in the windows of every bright red minivan in the lot before asking for help.) But I do try to recognize my weaknesses' worth. Strength tends to breed independence on my part. But weakness, in physical, mental, or spiritual form, cracks my shell of self-sufficiency and forces me to seek God.

I recently found this quote by Francis Frangipane—pastor, author, and founder of River of Life Ministries in Cedar Rapids, Iowa: "There will be no 'knights in shining armor' in God's kingdom; our armor will have many dings and dents. No, no perfect Hollywood heroes will ride to save the day; just wearied saints to look to God and, in weakness, find Christ's strength. This, indeed, is the essence of God's kingdom: divine greatness manifest in common people."

Divine greatness manifests in the weakness of common people. I wonder if the angels applaud with abandon every time it happens.

11 Our Little Corner of Redneckdom

She is clothed with strength and dignity.

Proverbs 31:25

As I said before, I am from the South. In my imagination, I am a cultured Southern belle who never leaves the house without makeup and has a closet dedicated to Kentucky Derby hats. I would like to live a life of dignified gentility. But it just isn't in my genes.

At a point in my past, I attempted Southern etiquette and decorum because I thought I could learn to live a dignified lifestyle. I pulled my wedding china out of the attic, stored it in a kitchen cabinet, and pretended I would use it one day. I included a knife and spoon in my table settings, even when I knew my family would not need them for the meal. I never wore white before Easter or after Labor Day. And I bought a pair of high-heeled shoes. (I couldn't walk in them, but they sat in my closet as a chic reminder of my new refined lifestyle.)

It was during that time my sister talked me into buying a subscription to a magazine that guaranteed its readers a more organized, sophisticated life. Her son was selling them in a school fund-raiser.

"The magazine is written for people like you," she said. "It is full of organizational tips for women looking to better their lives. It is just what you need."

So I wrote my check for $20, and my nephew inched one subscription closer to earning his bonus gift, the $2 flying saucer that doesn't fly but does require $10 worth of batteries to light up the sky with the voltage of an anemic firefly.

I received my first issue of the magazine within a few weeks. The cover looked good. "No More Clutter" stretched in black letters along the top followed by "Get Organized, Stay Organized," "Bug-Bite Remedies," and "5 Minute Summer Hair." Wow! No mess in my house, no frizz in my hair, no scratched-up mosquito bites to draw attention to the spider veins in my legs. That was just what I needed!

I sat down in my favorite reading chair to check out the issue. The table of contents was simple to follow, and the editor's article was about dealing with inadequacy. That was encouraging. The first ad featured a smiling, well-dressed, healthy-sized woman. No unrealistic size "skinny butt" was anywhere in the picture to make me feel excluded. I was beginning to think my sister had been right about the magazine. . . until I got to page 23.

On page 23 of the June 2012 issue, the editors of the magazine had printed organizing ideas that were sent to them by other subscribers and readers of *Real Simple* magazine, other people like me who were hoping to add organization and elegance to their lives. I read:

- "When my daughters were little, I would put together complete outfits, down to the hair clips, place them in large plastic bags, then stock their dressers."

- "I organized all my tablecloths by length and hung them on flocked hangers."
- "The narrow spice racks I installed inside my pantry doors hold approximately 75 spices, from A (achiote) to Z (za'atar).
- "I created a spreadsheet on which I write the title and author of every book I finish, along with a synopsis, the date I turned the last page, and a comment on how easy it was to get through."

What? Who are those people?!

Are there really people who have time to organize their children's clothes, including hair bows, and place them in bags to be arranged in drawers? When my kids were at home, I dressed them in anything I could find that was clean. If that plan failed, I pulled something out of the laundry hamper, shook out the wrinkles, and sniffed the armpits. If my eyes didn't water, it was good to go.

How does a woman own so many tablecloths she has to organize them by length to find one? I own two tablecloths. I know exactly where they are. The one I bought under the delusion that someday I would have the motivation to cook a big meal and set a beautiful table is hanging unused in a closet. The tablecloth from my childhood that I inherited from my mother is hanging on my windows as an answer to our kitchen's need for curtains.

Why would a person flock a hanger? What in the world are achiote and za'atar? And how can reading be organized on a spreadsheet and still be enjoyed as the lovely, lazy pleasure that it is?

Those people were not like me. Not at all. It turns out, my

sister's new magazine was not just what I needed. Evidently, I needed to give up my dreams of dignified Southern gentility and subscribe to something humbler than that. I needed a subscription to a magazine for women who want to feed their moderately clean families a meal seasoned with commonplace spices on a table set with half-finished art projects and plastic army battle scenes while they talk about a wonderful book they read at some unknown point in the past that was written by an author whose name they can't remember.

Although I have pretended otherwise, I knew from the beginning of my Proverbs 31 journey that a dignified lifestyle requirement would not work for me. A farcical form of indignity infests my family. I eventually learned to embrace it.

For several years, I have written in a blog and a local newspaper column stories about our plights. I was once asked by a lady who reads the blog if I make up the stuff I write or if it really happens. I answered her question by telling her about a predicament our family had experienced that week.

A year earlier, my oldest daughter had returned home after working in Thailand as a journalist to find that her car had died a loud and painfully expensive death and had been laid to rest in a junkyard where he was selflessly donating his used parts so other Mitsubishi Mirages could live. Casey was forced to either buy a cheap car or drive the 1990 Buick Century that had previously belonged to her ninety-two-year-old great-grandmother. The state of her bank account persuaded her to choose free over cheap, so for that year she drove an "old lady" car she named Miss Daisy. A few weeks before my reader's question, Miss Daisy had also kicked the oil bucket.

My husband was taught by his father, who was taught by his father before him, the Northcutt automotive philosophy: "Why spend money to buy a new car when you can hold an old one together with toothpicks and duct tape?" Greg had found Casey a used car that was to be delivered to our house as soon as the back half of its body had been replaced. The car had survived a wreck, which, according to its insurance company, had totaled it. But frugality told us that once a little superglue and a rubber band or two were applied, it would be just the car for our daughter. Until her new used car was ready, Casey had been forced to borrow a car from me or her younger brother, Peter.

Not long after Miss Daisy's passing, my oldest son, Ben, who has also been taught the Northcutt automotive philosophy, lost one of his family's minivans to ADD (needs mechanical Attention but owner has money Deficit Disorder). So Ben had borrowed Peter's car, leaving Casey, Peter, and me to share my minivan.

Then my minivan broke. At that point, Casey, Peter, and I were forced to share our farm vehicle, a souped-up diesel truck that smelled like a horse, made enough noise to drown out KISS in concert, and blew black smoke out the tailpipe. It was, at the time, loaded with tree limbs we had cleaned from our farm so our front yard would look r-e-e-eal nice for a fried catfish wedding reception, which was scheduled a few weeks from that day.

The truck had a stick shift. Casey and Peter could not drive a stick shift. So Casey, Peter, and I were sharing a vehicle that only I could drive.

On the morning of that particular predicament, Casey, who had been working as a freelance writer, had to cover a breakfast meeting of local government representatives. I got up at six a.m. to drive Casey to the meeting. The temperature was high so we drove the thirty miles with the windows down because the chewing gum that held in the air conditioner coolant had fallen off years before.

I dropped off Casey a block from the building that hosted her meeting. She didn't want the men in ties and the ladies in heels to see her repelling from the cab of a jacked-up truck her mother was driving. As she tumbled out of the truck, I heard her grumble something about a lack of professional behavior and an abundance of family embarrassment. Evidently, the Northcutt automotive philosophy runs recessive in her genes.

The truck and I spent the morning parked in an abandoned lot on the edge of town with an eight-foot concrete wall blocking us from the view of the men in ties and the ladies in heels. While we waited for the meeting to end and Casey to covertly find her way back to us, I put every word of that indignity into a humor blog for all to read.

After all, I am from the South. Sweating through a summer morning in a jacked-up truck parked on the banks of the Tennessee River is about as Southern as you can get.

Fortunately for me, when the writer of Proverbs 31 said the Virtuous Woman is clothed in dignity, he didn't mean elegance and etiquette. Most commentaries state that the strength and dignity mentioned in verse 25 are inner characteristics. The Geneva Study Bible calls them apparel of the Spirit. They were first seen in God Himself.

The Hebrew word that is translated "strength" in Proverbs 31:25 is attributed to God in Psalm 93:1. "The LORD reigns, He is clothed with majesty; The LORD has clothed and girded Himself with strength; Indeed, the world is firmly established, it will not be moved" (NASB).

The Hebrew word that is translated "dignity" in Proverbs 31:25 is translated "majesty" and attributed to God in Psalm 104:1. "Bless the LORD, O my soul! O LORD my God, You are very great; You are clothed with splendor and majesty" (NASB).

The strength and dignity of the Virtuous Woman are inner clothing, designed and modeled for her by God.

In the New Testament, Paul speaks to Christians about putting on the character of Christ. He tells the church at Colossae to clothe themselves with a list of spiritual characteristics.

> So, as those who have been chosen of God, holy and beloved, put on a heart of compassion, kindness, humility, gentleness and patience; Beyond all these things put on love, which is the perfect bond of unity. (Col. 3:12,14 NASB).

Paul writes as though putting on the character of Christ is easy. (It would be easier to put a swimsuit on Mona Lisa.) I have no idea how a woman in the Old Testament would have clothed herself with the attributes of God. But I have tried to become like Christ and have found there is only one way I can put on His character.

I got married in my mother's wedding dress. It had fitted sleeves, a hooped skirt, a sizable train, and a long row of buttons hiding a zipper in the back. I had to have help from my mother, my sister, and the seamstress who took in the bustline to get into the thing. It was too heavy to pick up and slip over my head. I couldn't zip up the dress without throwing my shoulders out of place. And if I had been forced to fasten all the tiny buttons by myself, I would have missed the wedding, the honeymoon, and the birth of my first child. So I raised my arms and let the other women slide it on and close it up.

When I read the verses about putting on the character of Christ, I feel like I'm in the same dilemma. I try to wrap compassion and kindness around my heart, but they won't stay. They continually come loose and fall down around my feet. I want people to see humility and gentleness in me, but the buttons that are supposed to hold them on keep popping off. When I most need patience, it gets caught in the zipper.

And the love of God? It is massive! I can't pick it up.

Try as I might, I can't put on the character of Christ or the attributes of God mentioned in Proverbs 31. But I can stand still, raise my arms like a child, and let the Holy Spirit pull them over my head and settle them into place.

12 Nine Big, Fat Fs and Jesus

A woman who fears the LORD is to be praised.

Proverbs 31:30

From the Southern Baptist Church that sits on a corner in my Bible Belt hometown, I learned that Jesus loves me. And this I know.

Because I learned this early in my childhood, I don't think I have ever feared the Lord as we define fear. However, I spent a significant part of my life fearing I would fail and disappoint Him. I was afraid He would not be pleased with me, that He would never say to me, "Well done, my good and faithful servant."

So I worked hard to be a good Christian. For a while I thought I was doing well. But when I sat down with the checklist we Christians have made for ourselves and took a realistic look at it, this is what I found.

The Top Ten Reasons I *Thought* I Qualified to Be a Good Christian

Number 10: Bible Study

I have studied the Bible for most of my life. Unfortunately, I have more questions now than when I started. It seems that the more I read, the less I know.

Fail.

Number 9: Bible Memorization

I have memorized Scripture in Sunbeams, GAs, Sunday school, youth camps, church services, and an extensive variety of Bible study groups. However, that bad case of I-can't-remember-anything-and-by-anything-I-mean-*everything* wiped out most of the memorization. The remnants of those verses are floating around in my mind, playing hide-and-seek with my memory retrieval.

Fail.

Number 8: Bible Drill Skills

Virtuous Woman Wannabes of my age who grew up in fundamental churches will remember Bible drills. As children, we stood in a line with our competitors, holding our Bibles, waiting for the drill leader to deliver the calls that would instruct us to locate a given verse. "Attention!" With that command, we snapped into place, holding our Bibles at our sides. "Present Bibles!" We raised our Bibles in our left hands and placed our right hands on top of them. At that point the drill leader gave us the Scripture reference followed by the last command. Then I threw open my

Bible and proceeded to beat the spiritual snot out of the other little kids before "Start" could be heard by the backsliders sitting on the last row of the church.

The Lord told me a few years ago that He never considered that to be a win.

Number 7: Stewardship

I have no problem giving God 10 percent of our income. It's giving him the other 90 that comes back to bite me in my "all about me" budget.

Big fat fiduciary fail.

Number 6: Quiet Time

Over the span of my VWW years, I often set aside times of disciplined Bible study and prayer. I have scheduled quiet times in my day from first thing in the morning to last thing at night, and held them under trees, on our porch, over my breakfast, in my favorite chair, and under the quilts of my bed. (Those tended to end a little early.) Although I had good intentions, I never could stick with them for an extended period of time.

I gave up structured quiet times a few years ago to hang out informally with the Holy Spirit.

Number 5: Taming my tongue to avoid inappropriate language

After giving up sewing for my spiritual health, I quit using bad language. My tongue was no longer tempted to throw out inappropriate four-letter words. That is until my children each turned sixteen and got a beginner's driving permit. They learned to drive a car and I learned to cuss again.

I failed the good Christian test and lost the Mother of the Year award at the same time.

Number 4: (For Women Only) Wives submitting to their husbands

Submitting to my husband in an area of disagreement is possible. Doing it without calling him a jerkface is not.

Failure in attitude

Number 3: Having the heart of a servant

I really don't mind helping out people…in my neighborhood… on Tuesdays from 6 to 8 p.m.…if it gets me out of cooking supper…and I can record my favorite television programs.

I'd say this one is "iffy" at best.

Number 2: Witnessing

If by "witnessing" you mean publicly stating strong Christian beliefs out loud to people I don't know. And if those people I don't know might want to talk to me further about religious stuff (or anything else), then as a card-carrying member of the shy and introverted club, I will fail, flop, flounder, and fold.

The Last-Ditch Reason I Qualify to be a Good Christian: Number 1: Jesus

It turns out I have nothing but Him.

In knowing Jesus, we can lose the fear of God's punishment. In learning to walk with the Holy Spirit, we can leave behind the fear of disappointing Him. But, for me, there is something much deeper, more spiritual in the concept of fearing the Lord.

According to the Holman Bible Dictionary, "Fear of God is not the dread that results from fear of punishment. Rather, it is to be understood as the reverential regard and the awe that comes out of recognition and submission to the divine." In further explanation it adds, "Most often the sense of fear comes as individuals encounter the divine in the context of revelation. When God appears to a person, the person experiences the reality of God's holiness."

Did you get that definition?

Fear of God is the reverential regard and awe that comes from recognition and submission to the divine.

Did you get how it happens?

Most often the sense of fear comes as individuals encounter the divine in the context of revelation.

A few years ago, my husband and I were given tickets to a James Taylor concert. It was the third time we had seen James in concert and, by far, the best. (I have never met James Taylor, so it may seem a bit presumptuous of me to call him by his first name, but I feel the pleasure his music has put in my life and the many dollars I have, in return, placed in his pocket have made it acceptable.)

With the first notes of the concert, I settled into the music, tapping my foot to the rhythm of James's guitar, which was dead on. Mine, not so much. But I tapped anyway as Greg and I sang along to all his old songs.

"In my mind I'm gone to Carolina. Can't you see the sunshine?

Can't you just feel the moonshine?"

I was gone. I could see the sunshine. I could soooo feel the moonshine.

For the next two hours, I was transfixed. The room filled with the sound of James Taylor's music. Then it filled with the beauty and aesthetic power of his music. Then, for me, it filled with the Creator of his music.

James may or may not recognize that God is the designer of his talent and the author of his music. But I surely do. The same artisan who carved the seas and laid them down beside the shores designed that voice and placed it in James Taylor. The same hand that paints a sunset guides the fingers on James Taylor's guitar. Beauty in all forms, even when disclosed by the unredeemed, springs from the hands of God, circles around His being, and resounds with His voice.

While James sang that night, God appeared in a realm just beyond the stage. I saw Him there. His presence was overwhelming. And my soul responded with reverence and awe.

I stuck my head out the window this morning
and spring kissed me bang in the face.

Langston Hughes

I love the colors of spring. They make my soul sigh with pleasure after a long, dreary winter. I have a forsythia bush near the end of my driveway that is always the first to bloom. When it begins to turn yellow, I know life is returning to my yard. The daffodils that line the fence pop up to sing in hundred-part harmony, "Ding dong the winter's dead. The winter's dead. The winter's dead. Ding dong the wicked winter's dead!" My trees blossom, my irises bloom, and all is right with my outside world.

I love the scents of spring. With the first warmth of the season, I open my doors to let it blow through my house. I inhale the scent of the rain and the grass and whiffs of the daffodils. Then I close my eyes and breathe deeper to smell the sun and the sky and the songs of the birds.

The Lord gave me a timid and reserved personality. My mother, with a lot of help from the yardstick in her hand and a little encouragement from my dad in the recliner, gave me a proper and disciplined upbringing. As a result, I am modest and meek in most things.

But when I stick my head out the door at the end of a cold, dead winter and a spring morning kisses me bang in the face, I kick off my shoes and dance. Like King David leaping with all his might before the Lord, like Snoopy jigging with his face raised to the sky, like the Rockettes giving Old Man Winter a kick in the behind, I dance.

Then I raise my hands to the sky and stand before God who has, once again, colored the world with life and has revealed Himself to me in the process. And my soul shouts with reverence and awe.

The Holman Bible Dictionary also says, "This self-disclosure of God (the revelation of Himself that causes reverence) points to the vast distinction between humans and God, to the mysterious characteristic of God that at the same time attracts and repels. There is a mystery in divine holiness that causes individuals to become overwhelmed with a sense of awe and fear."

Did you get why it happens?

There is a mystery in the holiness of God that causes us to be overwhelmed with a sense of awe and reverential fear. "And all that dwell upon the earth shall worship him, whose names are not written in the book of life of the Lamb slain from the foundation of the world" (Rev. 13:8 KJV).

I had an epiphany about this Scripture verse a few years ago. I have no idea how I could have gone to church for half a century, studied and color coded my Bible until it looked like psychedelic art from the '60s, and never before have seen the last phrase of this verse. "Slain from the foundation of the world."

I pondered that phrase for a long time. I read Bible commentaries and filled one of my husband's legal pads with research notes about it. Since the day those words first caught my attention, I have contemplated their significance. They gave birth to a powerful "what if" story that now lives in my imagination.

In the beginning, after God spoke all the "Let there be"s and creation formed at His commands, He paused to say, "Let us make mankind in our image, in our likeness, so that they may rule over the fish in the sea and the birds in the sky, over the livestock and all the wild animals, and over all the creatures that move along the ground." (Gen. 1:26)

What if after They spoke into being the magnificent and the

instinctual, God paused in creation and said to Jesus and the Spirit, who hovered with the Father and Son, "Let's talk about this before we go any further." With excitement in His voice, perhaps God said, "I'd like to make man. I'd like to breathe a bit of ourselves into him so that he will be different from the animals and we can love him more."

At this point in the story in my head, Jesus and the Spirit nod. It would be a little more complicated and they might get a little dirt on their hands, but what an intriguing idea! Then God becomes pensive and says, "But look down the road of time. If we create these people, look at the mess they will make. Watch their path as they follow their choices and see where we will go to retrieve them."

As the Spirit follows the path mankind will walk, He nods His assent. Yes, He will lead them through a desert. Yes, He will visit them in their promised land. He can be there to give courage as they battle. He will gladly comfort their kings and prophets in the days of their sorrow and cause them to dance in the days of their joy.

Then He looks forward a little more and sees the place in time where God will determine that mankind has wandered long enough without Him. And, if the Spirit has something like a heart, it stops beating for a moment when He realizes what making these people will cost. With effort, He pulls his eyes away from the cross and looks at Jesus.

Jesus is still. Breath seems to have left His body. He has seen too. But His eyes are not on the cross. They are on the Father. He stands there for what would have, if there had been time, seemed like eternity. He looks. And He sees. And He understands.

Then Jesus nods.

And from the foundation of the world, He is slain.

All I have is Jesus. And my soul cries in reverence and awe.

13 A Penny Saved Is a Penny Earned and Then Lost Somewhere in the Couch Cushions

She makes sure her dealings are profitable.
Proverbs 31:18 (NLT)

I can tell the type of day my husband had at work by what he watches on television when he gets home. A good day at his office means he is willing to watch a drama I choose. On a bad day, he needs to laugh. So our evening holds a lineup of half-hour comedies that require no mental activity. On the beyond-bad days, the days on which he wonders why he became an attorney and I wonder how many crowns God will give me for living with one, he watches reality TV. *Iron Chef America*, *Pawn Stars*, and *The Joy of Painting* with Bob Ross work for him on those days. He need not find the energy to laugh, and all his mind has to do is remember to breathe.

Recently, he came home on a beyond-bad day and we watched *Tiny House Nation* on FYI Network. On this reality television show, hosts John and Zack travel the country helping families design and construct mini-houses of 300 square feet, give or take a patio the size of a Twister mat.

We watched as John and Zack walked us through one of their tiny homes. The house was as cute as a smallish bug. Zack welcomed us into a spotless new home that had been professionally decorated with an eye toward creative storage and pleasing colors. Even the basket of fruit by the sink matched the colors in the wallpaper. It also took up half the counter space in the kitchen. Over Zack's head was a small bedroom balcony. The bed was neatly made and adorned with pretty, little pillows that drew your eye away from the closet, which was just big enough to hold Barbie's wardrobe.

My husband, who was having visions of quitting his job and selling everything that needs to be mowed, painted, or super-glued, was enthralled with the mini house. As the credits scrolled, he looked at me and asked, "How would you like to live in a tiny house?"

How would I like to live in a tiny house? Is the man crazy? I have lived in a tiny house. I have lived in a tiny house with him. I have lived in a tiny house with him, his parents, and all of our children.

When you have five kids, vacationing is expensive. When the kids get old enough to realize that in normal families kids don't sleep five to a double bed and you have to pay for two hotel rooms, vacations cost a small fortune. So for the years we were rearing several kids at the same time, we vacationed in a twenty-nine-foot motorhome. Many of our trips were taken with my in-laws because we liked to be generous with our vacation experiences. Also, because they actually owned the motorhome. As many as nine people in a mobile, miniature house, traveling across the country for weeks at a time. That is the way we vacationed for twenty years.

Our tiny house was not new or spotless, and the fruit on our counter usually just attracted ants. We slept on everything that would lie flat. Two slept in the bed in the back room. Two occupied the bed over the cab. Brothers slept together on the pulled-out couch. A daughter slept on the table. A son slept on the floor. The baby slept in a laundry basket beside the garbage can.

We did have an abundance of creative storage space. We had clothes stored in every crevice with a door. We kept shoes in the shower, toys in the oven, and guitars on either side of the bed in the back room. To get our clothes from the closet, we had to either crawl across the bed or send our most agile child to traverse the room, balanced on the edge of a guitar case.

I must admit that living in the motorhome brought about an unusual amount of closeness in our family. We were a well-choreographed unit when getting dressed in the morning. While one was doing what could only be done in the bathroom, the rest of us were adapting to the cramped space as we got ready for the day. The one who needed an electrical outlet to help with grooming sat on the bed, holding a curling iron between her knees, resting her feet on a guitar case, and throwing toiletries to those who called for them. Toothpaste went to the one at the kitchen sink. A hairbrush was tossed to the one primping before his or her reflection in the refrigerator door. Deodorant was sent to the one dressing in a prone position on the bed over the cab. Baby wipes flew over the one tying shoes on the couch and into the hands of the one changing a diaper on the kitchen table.

We also had great fun in our tiny house. I think that motorhome is where we learned to hug so much. We had no choice but to stand side by side and figure out what to do with our arms. They might as well have been wrapped around the one standing next to us. But as the person in charge of preparing meals, finding clean underwear, retrieving stored items, breaking up sibling fights, and forcing children to brush their teeth in a teacup-sized sink, all while holding my tongue so my kids did not hear me vent inappropriately at the guitar cases beside the bed, I also experienced some high levels of stress on those vacations.

Let me tell you what living with a large family in a motorhome is like. It always looks like a tornado rolled in the door and then out again, realizing it could do no more damage than had already been done. To get to the peanut butter, you have to unload the bread, chips, cereal boxes, all the Hostess snacks you bought to keep your kids happy while you travel, the cans of healthy stuff that will never be eaten, and the chocolate you have hidden in the back of the cabinet to get you through the trip. To get to the paper towel reserves, you have to move five people off the couch, wake the sleeping baby, lift the sofa seat, and crawl into the storage compartment. Once there, you have to dig through pots and pans, grilling utensils, mosquito candles, and mousetraps. To change into your pajamas at the end of the day, you have to tie the bedroom door closed, crawl across the bed to pull the shades, hang upside down to pull your PJs from under the guitar cases, and make sure your kids don't open the door and come face to naked face with emotional scarring.

Do I want to live in a tiny house? Not until senility sets in and I have no mind to lose.

But I did enjoy our vacations in the motorhome. That old thing took us on some wonderful trips that left us with enough money to afford family counseling when we got home. And if I could tie that motorhome back together with rubber bands and chewing-gum strings, I would load up my now larger family and drive it one more time.

… to a lodge that would hold us all in stress-free comfort.

Vacationing by motorhome is only one in a long line of frugal choices my husband and I have made for our family. Greg worked out our first budget the year we were married. He came to our marriage with an undergraduate degree in accounting, which made him good with financial numbers, and a family heritage of frugality that traced back to the 1700s when the first minted pennies were pinched by his Northcutt ancestors. It's a good thing he brought his frugal tendencies with him because during the first few years of our marriage, every penny counted. The second summer we were married, I paid tuition for college classes with the entirety of our checking account plus the spare change we kept in a saucer for use at the campus laundromat.

During the years we were rearing five children and our finances were tight, budgeting became second nature. We rented modest homes for the first ten years of our marriage to save a substantial down payment on our house. We bought used cars and drove them until they were held together with toothpicks and duct tape. We went clothes shopping at yard sales and low-end department stores, unless there was an occasion when my kids needed something more expensive. At those times, I dressed them in their most ragged, mismatched clothes and sent them to my sister's house. She gasped with mortification, threw them into her car, and took them shopping.

Profitable dealings? I can do those! It isn't hard for me to spend within our income. Extravagant possessions don't tempt me. Keeping up with the Joneses doesn't interest me much.

I truly believe the Lord is my shepherd and I shall not want for anything I need. I also believe the Lord is my shepherd and I shall not want for more than He has given me. I shall not want a fashionable, freshly painted home when He has given me a farmhouse that is simple and lovingly worn. I shall not want a husband who gives me expensive gifts when He has given me a man who sings me love songs. I shall not want reservations at the Ritz-Carlton when He has given me a night with friends by a campfire.

Does that information about me sound like it would meet a Proverbs 31 standard? It does, doesn't it? Does it qualify as a good work of a Virtuous Woman? It seems like it might. Is God impressed with it? I think that is a complicated question.

A person in my life was a bug in my britches for years. He rubbed me wrong for a long time. I didn't talk about it to anyone because Virtuous Woman Wannabes shouldn't harbor resentment toward people. I didn't think about it often because I hoped if I ignored the discord I felt, I could respond with feigned ignorance when the Holy Spirit pointed it out.

However, the Spirit, being one-third of an all-knowing deity, didn't believe my ignorance excuse and convicted me of a lack of love and a general bad attitude. So I began to pray for patience. It took a while but there eventually came a day when I responded to that person in love rather than resentment. I don't mean that I chose an act of kindness. I mean that there was a genuine change in my attitude.

I had done it! I had let the Holy Spirit do a spiritual work in me and I was excited about it. I was also eager to point it out to God. "Look, Lord! Look what I did! I let You work in me and I loved like Jesus would. The resentment is gone and there is a hole where that sin used to be."

God leaned over my shoulder and whispered in my ear. "Yes, child, I see the hole. And now I see spiritual pride rushing in to fill it up."

Well, crap! When He pointed it out, I saw it too.

You would think that after knowing Jesus for forty-five years, I would be better at avoiding sin. Some days I think I am improving. Other days, I know I am not. You would think that after seriously walking with Jesus for over thirty years, I would be better at producing good works and loving attitudes. How good can my works be if they leave me treading water in a pool of spiritual pride? Is there anything in that scenario that is impressive to God? I honestly don't know.

With a big hallelujah and a little dance of praise, I thank God that it doesn't matter. My life with Him is not about whether or not I avoid sin or accomplish good works, financial or otherwise, and that is my sanctifying salvation. Because, by those standards, even when I succeed, I fail.

We must not remove our eye from looking alone to Jesus
Himself even to adore his image within ourselves; for if
we do so, we shall go backward rather than forward.

Charles Spurgeon

14 Unmasked by a Homeless Guy and a HoneyBaked Ham

*She extends a helping hand to the poor
and opens her arms to the needy.*

Proverbs 31:20 (NLT)

If you grew up in a church, you saw women extend their hands to the poor. If you grew up in a small-town Southern church, those hands were probably holding a cake plate and a casserole dish. Caring for others, whether feeding a pot roast to the poor in body or wrapping arms around the poor in spirit, is what Christian women do.

Score one for this Virtuous Woman Wannabe! I may not meet many of the other standards of Proverbs 31, but the Christian women in my life have taught me how to serve. By opening her arms to the poor in our community, my mother taught me that a smile and a kind word are precious gifts to a lonely heart. With the work of her hands, my mother-in-law taught me a simple loaf of bread given in love can soothe a soul in pain. My Virtuous Woman mentors taught me the gifts of food and child care can lighten the load of a young mother. And the dear women of our previous church family, who offered their hands to me during two of my pregnancies when health issues kept me immobile for many months, taught me there is no better way to love a woman than to care for her family.

Pretty impressive, don't you think? I had this Proverbs 31 trait tied up and securely stored in my VWW Conference bag early in my adult life.

At least, I had it in the bag until the ham incident of 2014.

It happened the week before Christmas when I was beyond busy. On this particular day, I was running late...again. I was headed to an appointment with my beautician because no middle-aged woman wants the roots of her hair to shine brighter than the tree lights in the family Christmas pictures.

As I drove up the main street of our little town, singing *The Christmas Song* with James Taylor on the radio, I glanced toward my husband's law office. I saw two boxes sitting on the porch. I had received a notification from Amazon saying the theology books I had ordered for my nephew's Christmas present had been delivered. So I knew what was in the smaller box. I slowed down as I approached the building and squinted at the larger box. "What in the world?...Hey, maybe...Could it be?...I think it might...Yes, it is!...Hallelujah!...It's my HoneyBaked Ham!"

Give me a few seconds to tell you about my HoneyBaked Ham. This is no ordinary ham. It is a fine, lean specimen of pork, marinated in a sauce made with Christmas magic, smoked over hardwood chips, topped with a smack-your-mama, sweet sauce, and spiral sliced for my convenience. A longtime client sends the ham to my husband every Christmas, and it is so good your mama will turn the other cheek when you slap her as long as you share a slice or two with her.

That ham is delicious. But there is oh so much more to it than the way it tastes. Because our family Christmas meal is traditionally shrimp, I freeze the ham and serve it on the following Thanksgiving. Thanksgiving is, by far, the biggest of the sit-down meals in our extended family. The absurd abundance of food on the table is exceeded only by the crazy amount of preparation time spent in the kitchen. Ownership of that ham (which, by the way, I simply thaw and serve) gives me the ability to assign the purchasing, storing, preparing, baking, and carving of the turkey to my sister-in-law.

I love that ham.

It was late in coming that December, and I had begun to worry about it. But from the car window, I could see it was sitting on the office porch. James Taylor was singing carols through my radio. The town around me was celebrating the season with holiday spirit. All was well with my Christmas.

My husband's office was closed that day for one of his many out-of-office holiday experiences. (The man knows how to enjoy the season.) I thought for a moment that I should stop and pick up the packages. But, as I said, I was late for my appointment. And, as I thought then, what could happen in the middle of the day in my small, Kentucky town, home to 2500 good-hearted people who were celebrating the birth of Jesus and sending one another Christmas cards that say, "Hey, Y'all, Peace on Earth Today"? So, I drove past my husband's office, leaving my nephew's books and my HoneyBaked Ham on the porch.

An hour and a half later, when I drove back to pick up the boxes, they were gone.

I couldn't comprehend what I was seeing or, rather, what I was not seeing. Gone? How could the boxes be gone? Who in our small-town, America, would steal a neighbor's Christmas packages? And what dim-witted citizen would take them from the porch of the city attorney's office?

I was stunned. I was confounded. I was furious. Some low-down, no-account Christmas grinch had taken my ham!

My one consolation was that the thief had also taken two books about Christian theology. I hoped they would smote him with guilt and condemnation. If I could have gotten hold of him, I would have smote him with a few other things.

I wrote my anger on my Facebook page that night, "I love HoneyBaked Ham and they don't come cheap! Oh, Christmas thief, I have but a few words for you. My mother would expect me to keep the others to myself. YOU HAD BETTER BE HOMELESS AND HUNGRY! Otherwise, I want my ham back!"

I might have overreacted at that point. But in one act of Christmas crime, the wholesome shine on my small-town community was tarnished, Thanksgiving 2015 was severely compromised, and some lousy homeless guy had my ham. Ironically, the lousy homeless guy did not have to take it. I would have given my ham to a hungry man if he had asked.

I would have given my ham to a hungry man if he had asked.

Stop right here.

Do you see Him? At this point in the story, I ran smack-dab into Jesus. And I stumbled all over that last thought. Not because it isn't true. It is. I absolutely would have given away the ham to a person who needed it. I would have given it away quickly and easily with a cheerful heart and very little regret.

It seems that was actually the problem. If I could cheerfully give away my ham, why was I so angry because someone had taken it? Either way, my ham was gone and I would have a hand crammed up a turkey butt the following Thanksgiving. As Jesus pointed out to me, the lousy homeless guy in my imagination had taken more than my ham. He had also taken the opportunity for me to give it to him, to do a kindness for a person less fortunate, and to feel good about myself.

Do you see the problem? In both scenarios, my ham was gone and a hungry man had been fed. But in the first, the ham was taken from me and I was furious. In the second, I gave away the ham and I felt good about myself. Evidently, even in an act of generosity I am mostly about me.

Well, crapfire!

Like my expectations concerning sin and good works, I thought I was getting better at dying to my own desires so I could care for the needs of other people. And like my bout with spiritual pride, I saw my selfishness when Jesus pointed it out.

I plopped down in the puddle of self-condemnation that had pooled at my feet and wondered how I would ever get better if I kept stumbling over myself as I walked. Jesus sat down beside me and the puddle dried up. (There is no condemnation in His presence.) He told me not to waste time worrying about it because life with God is not about getting better.

Mother Teresa died in September 1997. Although she was globally recognized as a Catholic humanitarian, having received the Nobel Peace Prize in 1979 for her work among the poorest of the poor, her death received little notice on the American news and morning talk television shows. The majority of their news coverage that week centered around Princess Diana, who had been killed five days earlier in a dramatic car crash. The lack of publicity seemed sadly fitting for a woman who had spent much of her life working among lepers, an ostracized and unseen element of society, and who had refused to take personal credit for her accomplishments, claiming she was simply a tool in God's work.

However, on the day after Mother Teresa's death, I saw one video segment about her life and ministry on *The Today Show*. The correspondent did a short, biographical piece, which was followed by a few polite, generic remarks by a cardinal in the Catholic Church who said very little about the heart of the woman known among the poor as the Saint of the Gutters. Then the segment featured a young priest who had worked beside Mother Teresa as she gave spiritual comfort while caring for the medical needs of a colony of lepers in India.

The priest briefly described the symptoms of leprosy and explained the horrific nature of the medical treatment Mother Teresa performed daily on patient after patient within the colony. Then he spoke of a conversation he'd had with the nun as he observed her work. Amazed at her ability to clean and care for the putrid skin sores caused by the disease, the priest told her he would not do what she was doing for a million dollars. According to the priest, she looked up from bending over the sores and said, "I wouldn't do it for a million dollars either. I do it for Jesus."

Mother Teresa's reply has stayed with me for years, "I do it for Jesus." What a beautiful description of a Christian life. For me, those five simple words, without a theological jot or tittle among them, have come to characterize Christianity. Life with God is about choosing a path of obedience because Jesus beckons to us from that direction not because we are trying to avoid sin. It is about choosing the ways of a disciple because Jesus has called us to them not because we are trying to accumulate good deeds. And life with God is choosing to extend our hands to the poor not because we want to be better Christians, but because when we reach out to the least of people, we touch Jesus.

A note to those who are wondering how the ham incident ended: As it turned out, a few hours after depositing the boxes containing the ham and my nephew's books, the UPS man drove back by my husband's office. When he noticed the boxes were still on the porch, he picked them up again. The following day, he re-delivered them to the office.

I wrapped the theology books and gave them to my nephew Christmas Eve. I thawed and served the HoneyBaked Ham for our next Thanksgiving meal. My sister-in-law, once again, was assigned the purchasing, storing, preparing, baking, and carving of the turkey. In my next Facebook post, with wiser and kinder words, I apologized to the fictional thief for my bad attitude.

15 The Parable of the Best Cartoon Mother

Her worth is far above jewels.

Proverbs 31:10 (NASB)

A few years ago, I took a Facebook quiz to see which Disney mother I am most like. I thoughtfully answered a series of questions, and a Disney-illustrated computer program analyzed my answers. The program determined I am most like Sarabi, the mother lion in *The Lion King*. As a Sarabi-type mom, I am a gracious mother with a calm exterior and a fierce spirit.

Calm? Yep, that's me. Gracious and fierce? Well, those are not words I would have chosen to describe myself, but who am I to argue with an objective, scientific, Disney-animated personality quiz?

Based on the ten questions I answered in the thirty-eight seconds of self-analysis it took to take the test, a virtual analyst wrote this about me: "You would put yourself through hell and back for your family and never ask for a single thing in return which kind of makes you a saint."

A saint!

Me? Really?

No…well, maybe…okay…so, how can I argue with that? It is, after all, Facebook official. Let's see the other Disney mothers in the quiz do better than that!

Is Queen Elinor from *Brave* a better mother than Sarabi and me? Not likely. She may be a noble role model and have great hair, but her daughter has a rebellious streak and the triplets need to be locked in the dungeon until the sugar wears off.

Andy's mom from *Toy Story*? I don't think so. The quiz praises her for fostering creativity in her children, but did you get a good look at her house? There are toys *everywhere*!

Cinderella's Fairy Godmother? Not on her best day! Take away her magic wand and all she has to offer is a couple of rodents, a large vegetable, and a nonsensical song about an old biddy with boppity boobs. That is totally inappropriate for young children!

Who are the best Disney mothers? I think it is obvious that it is those of us who have a Sarabi-like philosophy of child rearing. But it doesn't matter what I think. To know who is the best Disney mom, we would have to ask Walt Disney.

Women are born with a need to know they are significant, that who they are and what they do is good and right and worthy. For those of us who are wives and mothers, it is often hard for us to find our worth. No one sends us memos that say, "Thumbs up on the aesthetically pleasing color variations in the foods on your dinner plates," or "Good job with the kitchen floor potty clean-up." Our jobs do not offer us plaques to hang on our walls or trophies to set on our shelves. We don't have standardized specifications by which we can measure our successes and feel good about ourselves. So we make up our own standards, and most of us are crazy hard on ourselves.

We must feed our families three healthy meals a day, preferably of our own making. We should love and honor our husbands and keep words like *jerkface* to ourselves. We must teach our children to work hard, obey instructions, and eat the green stuff on their plates. We need to make sure they do not to lie, steal, bully, or pick their noses in public. Our homes need to be in spit-shined order. Our bodies need to be in toned-up shape.

Many of us believe we have to meet these standards on our own because asking for help is a sign of weakness. Using the television as a babysitter so we can shower, brush our teeth, clean the maple syrup off the toilet seat, and keep the family in clean underwear would cost us points in our quest to be the most conscientious of mothers. Two consecutive meals of frozen help from Mrs. Smith or the people over at Pepperidge Farm and we would leave the diligent homemaker's club in disgrace.

At some point, we realize it is impossible to meet all the requirements we set for ourselves. We must accept failure or set priorities. Each of us chooses the issues we consider to be most important in our quest to be good wives and mothers, and we adopt philosophies of what is right and what is wrong about each of them. Among others, these issues include:

- Determining whether or not we should work outside our homes
- Respecting and honoring our husbands
- Disciplining and schooling our children
- Spiritual training of our children
- Food and health choices for our families

When we have chosen our issues and determined our philosophies, we find other women who have made the same choices, and we group ourselves with them, finding confidence and strength in numbers. Standing in the safety of our faction, we measure it against other groups of women, scrutinizing and judging them for their choices.

We determine that if the life choices of other wives and mothers are different from ours, they must be wrong. Because if they are right, it means we are wrong. And if we are wrong, we have failed in our roles and have no worth as a woman.

Early in my years as a wife and mother, I realized that my place in life would be as a woman who does not work outside her home. Although I am on the serious side of domestically challenged, I made that role choice and took a seat among the full-time homemakers. I rested in the knowledge that my choice was pleasing to the Lord. My understanding of Proverbs 31 made it clear that a Virtuous Woman Wannabe devotes all her time to her family and household. I tended to judge women who had made other choices, knowing that mine were good and right and worthy.

Morgan was a wife and mother who worked as a physician's assistant in our community. She was in the Sunday school class my husband and I taught, and we became friends. At the time, Morgan was young in her knowledge of God, sometimes doubting that she knew Him at all. There was a lot I wanted to teach her about the way God loves his children.

One Sunday morning, Morgan told our class about a woman who came into the clinic where she worked. The woman visited their clinic often, always dirty and smelling as though she had not bathed in weeks but was very seldom actually sick. Morgan was sure she just wanted to talk to someone.

None of the nurses or doctor's assistants wanted to take the woman into an examining room, shutting themselves in with the filth and body odor. They passed her around each time she visited the clinic until someone reluctantly examined her. That week it had been Morgan's turn.

Morgan took her unwashed patient to a room, closed the door and began to listen to the woman recite a list of aches and pains she more than likely did not have. As the woman talked, Morgan found herself listening to the woman's words and, for the first time, hearing loneliness in her voice. Morgan examined the woman's appearance with more observant eyes and saw a terrible sadness in her face.

As my friend sat in the examining room, intense compassion for that unwanted woman washed over her. Morgan didn't know why she was suddenly overcome with emotion, and she didn't know how to respond to it. All she could think to do was to wrap her arms around the unloved woman and hold her for a good long while.

When the story ended, our Sunday school class was an emotional mess. The men were engaged in a macho attempt to blink away the dampness in their eyes. The women had surrendered to their tears and drenched a box of Kleenex tissues.

I was both moved by Morgan's story and envious of her experience. I knew it had been the Holy Spirit who had flooded her with compassion that day. And He had done it in a way I had never experienced because, for the most part, my roles as a wife and mother kept me insulated from people like her unwanted woman. God had worked through Morgan to minister to one of the broken of the world because she had chosen a life that put her there among them. Although I intersect with people who are lost and in need of hope, I don't live among them like Morgan does. She will see God work in ways I will not. I came to understand that Morgan's choices and experiences in the world were good and right and worthy. She had a lot to teach me about the way God loves His children.

Pondering Morgan's story changed me. I continue to believe my role in the world is as a full-time wife and mother. But I no longer give thought to whether it is the right or wrong choice for every Virtuous Woman Wannabe, and I no longer judge its worth. I know it is the role God has given to me. If other women want to know if it is God's choice for them, I figure they can ask Him themselves.

Over the years, I have walked the path to God alongside women who came with principles and life choices in many different shapes and sizes. I have seen Him in all of them. My friend KariAnne doesn't cook. Her family lives on mac and cheese as well as pizza carried out from the nearest gas station. And she laughs about life and calls her friends rock stars and reminds us all that God thinks we are amazing.

Marla married her law-student husband a week after I married mine. She was my first newlywed friend and likely will be my last nursing home crony. When her children went to school, she chose to work outside her home. And unlike me and most VWWs of my generation, Marla didn't breastfeed her babies. And her heart beats with the spiritual gift of service. She shows me the hands of Jesus at work.

I have put in a housing request for my heavenly mansion to be built between the ones belonging to my friends Jen and Lynn. We want to spend eternity as next-door neighbors. The three of us differed on the appropriate way to educate our children. (Mine went to public school. Lynn's enrolled in a private, Christian school. Jen homeschooled her kids.) But we have spent thirty years reminding one another that God holds all of our children safely in the palms of His hands.

Bethany doesn't talk about the importance of teaching children to study the Bible. She has shown me the significance of teaching children to listen to the voice of the Holy Spirit.

Barb divorced her husband. And her prayers are mighty. They ring through the throne room of God.

As I have gotten older, the black-and-white edges of what is right and what is wrong for a VWW have blurred. At age over-forty, and by over-forty I mean somewhere upwards of fifty, my eyes will barely focus, and I don't see our differences like I used to. My hearing, however, is still pretty good. When I listen to women talk about Jesus with the same awestruck yearning I feel, I know we are walking the same path of grace.

I have no idea what Walt Disney would say if we could ask him who is the best of his Disney mothers. But if we were to ask God to identify the best of His Christian wives and mothers, I'm pretty sure I know how He would respond.

He would say, "Come to me, all of you women who have burdened yourselves with questions about who is right and who is wrong, and I will give you rest from all that crap" (Matt. 11:28, author's loose translation).

"Be still and know that you don't need to measure yourselves against one another, because I paid a terrible price to declare all of you good and right and worthy."

16 When the Winds of Winter Huff and Puff

When it snows, she has no fear for her household;
for all of them are clothed in scarlet.

Proverbs 31:21

Few people celebrate Christmas like Northcutts celebrate it. The whole lot of them are born with an excessive love for the holiday. It is in their genetic makeup. They begin counting down the days to the Christmas season somewhere around the first of January. Their countdown is shorter than most because, for those born with this surname, the Yuletide celebration begins in September. Those of us who marry into the family try to put a lid on the Christmas crazy with common, traditional practices, but that's like trying to dam Niagara Falls with a package of Pixie Stix.

For me and most other mothers, the excitement of the holiday season comes with a sleigh load of stress. While carols are proclaiming that peace and goodwill have come to men, women are adding the tasks of holiday traditions to their lists of things to do and multiplying the whole thing by the power of insanity. Peace for us? At Christmas time? Not likely.

When I had five young children to herd through the holiday, the Christmas season took the crazy of my normal day, wrapped it up with a strand of stress, and tied a big frazzled bow on top. Now that I have two dozen celebrants around my Christmas tree, give or take a dog or two, the season tears into my days and strews chaos through the month of December. Peace is usually delivered to somebody else's house.

But there was a year. A Christmas when peace found me. A year when Christmas peace surprised me at the IGA grocery store.

It happened around 10 p.m. on the night before we were to celebrate Christmas with my siblings and their families. I had taken a break from wrapping presents and spit-polishing my house to make a last-minute run to the grocery. The store was ten minutes from closing, and I was sprinting through the aisles, searching frantically for a can of oysters. It had been a particularly chaotic Christmas, and my stress level was soaring. I did not have time to play hide-and-seek with a can of oysters. I needed to grab the stupid thing and take it home to star as the main ingredient in my family's traditional oyster casserole.

Neither my siblings nor I like oyster casserole, but it is the dish our mom cooked for our dad every Christmas of our childhood. We were pretty sure Christmas dinner could not happen without it. It had been several years since our parents had been at our holiday table, but the casserole would sit there as a memorial to both of them…if I could find just one can of oysters!

As I hunted through the cans of tuna, shrimp, and sardines, I heard myself panicked and praying, "Lord, I need oysters!

"Just one can! Just one, Lord!

"It's okay if they are expired! We aren't going to eat them anyway!

"Lord, help me! I need a can of oysters!"

Then I found it! I found the can I needed and my prayers became thanksgiving.

"Thank You, Lord! Thank You! Thank You! Thank You! Christmas is complete!"

I realize that is a bit dramatic, but I blame it on fatigue…which disappeared with a new thought.

"Christmas! Oh, crap! It's almost Christmas, Lord, and the only thing I have thanked You for is a can of oysters. I've let the whole season go by without stopping to acknowledge or celebrate the birth of Jesus."

Suddenly, along with the stress that had dogged my days throughout the holiday season, I was piggybacking guilt, failure, and self-condemnation. It was a heavy load, and I was buckling under the weight.

How could I have completely ignored the fact that Christmas is about the Nativity? Did I not stop to read the Christmas cards as I signed them? Was I so distracted by the tasks of the holiday that I tuned out every Christmas carol? Had I become so complacent in the gift of grace that I had forgotten to be thankful for its beginning?

Then it happened. God came down to meet me in the canned goods aisle of the grocery store, and He said, "Child! You need to chill! It's okay. So you haven't thanked Me for the Nativity. And you mentally reviewed your shopping list during every sermon in December. And you didn't bake Jesus a birthday cake. And you fell asleep before Linus recited the Christmas story to Charlie Brown. I don't care. You hung on to the hem of My robe just to survive the season and you never let go. You did good."

God spoke. And there it was! My soul had found it for a moment. Christmas peace.

Why would the writer of Proverbs 31 say a Virtuous Woman does not fear snow because her household is clothed in scarlet? Day lands, I had no idea.

As a Virtuous Woman Wannabe, I needed to either exchange all my family's long johns for red union suits with the flaps in the back or find background information that would give another explanation to verse 21 and save my family some major embarrassment in the winter months.

In researching the Virtuous Woman passage, I found that commentaries have two explanations for the reference to clothing a household in scarlet. One explanation is that because the Hebrew language is written without vowels, the word translated "scarlet" actually could be a word that means "double." In fact, some versions of the Bible translate verse 21 to say the Virtuous Woman is not afraid of winter because her family has a double layer of clothing. The other explanation is that the term "scarlet" referred to the best quality of cloth. It would have been wool, which is a thick, warm material. And the brilliant red color would have given the cloth a stately, dignified appearance.

Either way, the writer of Proverbs 31 declared that a Virtuous Woman is prepared for the snow and cold weather of winter.

I keep two big plastic storage containers of miscellaneous gloves, scarves, hats, earmuffs, and face covers in the coat closet by our front door. At the first drop of winter's snowflakes, my children rummaged through those containers and bundled themselves up for outdoor play. My oldest usually choose to wear the full-face mask and matched it with his dad's old ski gloves and a long stocking hat with a little ball that hung down his back and waved in the wind when he sledded. His brothers, whom I had to force to wear hats and gloves, grabbed their choices quickly, without paying much attention to what they were doing. Their gloves were likely to be holey, mismatched, and two sizes too big.

I wanted my girls to be warm. I layered them with winter accessories of every kind and color. The thin, underlayer gloves in a dingy shade of green. The cute pink padded gloves. The old blue gloves that were handed down from their brothers. The red, black, or purple face covers. The long white scarf with holes in it. Any one of the sock hats with giant pom poms on top. And the hand-knitted ear cover that was lovely to look at but gave its wearer a headache because it fit too tightly.

My kids could be dressed and out the door, with their dad following in his Carhart coveralls, to sled before the snow got good and settled on the ground. Although there was not a thread of a stately or dignified piece of cloth to be found anywhere on their persons, my household was prepared for snow. We were ready in our own gaudy, disorganized, messy kind of way.

Symbolically, winter seasons represent the painful periods of life. Sometimes they are mild. Sometimes they blow in with gale-force winds. Either way, spiritually cold and emotionally dark days come to all of us. Viewing verse 21 of the Virtuous Woman passage from this perspective means a VWW needs to prepare her family for the times in life when circumstances are hard.

I wish I had neat, clear-cut answers to the questions my children ask when they are in pain. But I don't. Like the contents of the plastic storage containers in my coat closet, the insights I have to give my children about the difficult and painful things of the world are disorganized and messy.

From what I have seen, God gives jobs and He takes them away. Relationships come and go. Some of the broken ones are restored and some come to an angry end. Some illnesses are healed on this side of heaven; some on the other. Sometimes dementia takes a mind long before death takes a body. Children die. Abuse happens. Violence perpetuates itself.

Life can be hard and hurtful and grueling and piercing and oftentimes unbearable. With peace nowhere in sight.

Unless we hear the words of Jesus.

In the second year of Jesus's ministry, a crowd gathered on a mountain near the Sea of Galilee to hear Him speak. For the most part, they were Jews, the people God had chosen to be His own. Their nation had been under Roman rule for over sixty years, living in constant fear of Roman violence and cruelty.

The Jews had been waiting for generations for God to deliver them from persecution. They had reminded one another during all those years that one day He would end their suffering.

"Next year in Jerusalem!" They told one another day after day and season after season. "Next year in Jerusalem, God will send Messiah to help us!"

As they gathered that day, they had good reason to believe Jesus was the One God had sent. He had performed miracles and supernatural signs everywhere He went. Surely, He was the

Messiah God had promised would end their oppression. But Jesus had been with them for over a year and nothing had changed for the Jewish people.

I'm sure there were some in the crowd who were angry because God had promised them better than He had delivered and were tired of waiting for Jesus to make life easier. I imagine they stood in the back of the crowd as others gathered close around Him.

Most days, when I go to Jesus, I draw close to Him too. I sit at his feet and breathe in His words. But there have been days when I stood back with the angry ones, demanding of Him, "Are you the Messiah? Or are you not? Because if you are, you need to step up and fix some things!"

Jesus opened his mouth and spoke. He was talking to those of us who were sitting at his feet. But He spoke with enough force to reach those of us standing in the back of the crowd.

Blessed are the poor in spirit, for theirs is the kingdom of heaven.

Blessed are those who mourn, for they will be comforted.

Blessed are the meek, for they will inherit the earth.

Blessed are those who hunger and thirst for righteousness, for they will be filled.

Blessed are the merciful, for they will be shown mercy.

Blessed are the pure in heart, for they will see God.

Blessed are the peacemakers, for they will be called children of God.

Blessed are those who are persecuted because of

righteousness, for theirs is the kingdom of heaven. (Matt. 5:3–10)

His words were poignant and poetic, but few of the people on the mountain understood what they meant. How could they? He was speaking a spiritual language their physical ears could not interpret. But those of us on this side of the cross can hear the words of Jesus with spiritual ears. We can understand that the painful and humble places of life are where we most often see God. And that seeing God is our greatest blessing.

Before His crucifixion, Jesus sat down with His disciples and gave them His last instructions. Among them were these words:

> But the Comforter, even the Holy Spirit, whom the Father will send in my name, he shall teach you all things, and bring to your remembrance all that I said unto you. Peace I leave with you; my peace I give unto you: not as the world giveth, give I unto you. Let not your heart be troubled, neither let it be fearful. (John 14:26–27 ASV)

Jesus knew difficult circumstances were ahead for those at the table with Him. So He promised them a Comforter. He did the same for us. When we walk through hard and hurtful times in life, when we are troubled and fearful, the Holy Spirit is there to remind us of the words of Jesus and to speak to us the words of God.

"Child, it's okay. Open your spiritual eyes and see Me here. I will bring you mercy for today. I will draw you to My side and give you comfort. It is in this place that you most need Me, so it is in this place I will most fill you. It is here you can claim what I have promised you. It is here you become like Me.

"Child, it's okay. Don't run from this place. Here, where you are weak and humble, I bless you with Myself."

According to *Strong's Exhaustive Concordance of the Bible*, the Greek word translated "blessed" in the passage in Matthew means "happy or to be envied." When I am preparing my children for the winter seasons of life, I wrap them in the words of Jesus and suggest that when they are walking through difficult circumstances, they are to be envied rather than pitied. During the times when God's people are in the most pain, we are most likely to seek Him.

And the peace we find in His presence, the peace Jesus left for us warms us in the seasons of winter.

17 All This for a Swing on a Porch on a Farmhouse on a Hill

She smiles at the future.

Proverbs 31:25 (NASB)

My clumsy journey of domesticity began when I made a promise to a freckled, red-headed man who sang a love song to my forehead because he knew he would cry if he looked me in the eye. I wore my mother's wedding dress, and he, when he thought the timing was appropriate, wore a fake arrow through his head. At the end of that day, he took my hand and we ran through the arms of our families and friends. We drove away from our separate pasts to build a place that would be ours together. At the time, I had no idea where the road to that place would take us.

I didn't know we would suffer newlywed poverty, that our first home would be the dilapidated trailer with a cockroach population or that cooking in its kitchen would mean thawing the freezer with a hair dryer once a week and propping a chair against the stove to keep the oven door closed. I didn't know our bank account would routinely dwindle and dry up and I would appear at my college bursar's office to pay tuition with an assortment of bills and a handful of quarters I had pilfered from the laundry money jar.

I had no idea our final home would be a farmhouse styled with a dramatic, country-redneck flair. I didn't know about the dozens of dogs or the wandering sheep, geese, and chickens. The Thanksgiving turkey, the live-in pig, or the baby raccoon that was with us for just a few days but left an odor that still resides deep inside our nasal passages. The cows, the horses, or the proud, regal cat that would rule them all from the welcome mat at our front door.

I didn't know I would stand awkwardly at the helm of those homes, steering my family through life with a sizable amount of inattention and more than a little incompetence. I couldn't see that I would hate to sew, flounder as a cook, give up on vegetable gardening, and tend to forget where I left my children. From day one of my domestic life, meeting the conventional standards of the Proverbs 31 Virtuous Woman has been way beyond my skill set.

As I look back and see myself stumbling through my VWW years, feeling scatterbrained and slightly incompetent, I remember that time after time God met me along the way and, as during the Christmas hunt for oysters, He said, "Child! You really need to chill."

God knew exactly where the road would take the two of us when He sent me to the college where Greg Northcutt and his guitar were making music. On our journey together, we may have lurched along at times because Greg was tapping the gas pedal to a rhythm in his head. We may have serpentined occasionally because I was distracted by something on the side of the road. But He was directing us the whole time.

God was leading us here. To the place that is ours. To the farmhouse on the hill. To the front porch swing where Greg and I sit, holding hands and looking out over the life God has given us.

We talk about how grateful we are as we sit here, leaning back and enjoying the view of the flower beds in our yard and the animals in our fields. Then we turn in our seats, look over our shoulders, and savor life on the other side of the window, because our home holds the best of what we have been given.

Benjamin is our oldest child. He was born to us when we thought we could get the parenting thing right. He then set out to prove us wrong. As a kid, he was strong-willed and stubborn. He looked me in the eye and stepped over every line of obedience I drew. There were days I wanted to pinch off his head and tell Greg he up and died.

But on other days, he picked me flowers or played me songs on his Fisher-Price guitar, and his big eyes and pageboy haircut melted my heart. Always a pretender, he delighted me with the stories in his head. One day he was a knight with tales to tell of dragons and wizards. The next, a pirate with a bad brogue and a plastic sword, wearing an eyepatch and chasing his sibling enemies.

Ben became our most outgoing, gregarious personality. He laughs the loudest, parties the heartiest, and makes a friend of every stranger he meets. A musician like his dad, he plays guitar and adds a soft harmony to Greg's voice. When the two of them sing together, my heart puddles down around my feet.

Always a deep thinker, Ben earned a PhD in Family Ministry. He became a minister of youth and children, and parties for a living now. He married Jessica and brought her into the family. She sat down among us like she was born to be here and I love her a lot. Ben now has four of the world's most precious children who sing and pretend things and step over his lines of obedience. They make me glad I didn't pinch off his head when I had the hankering.

Casey was born before Benjamin turned two. She cried continually for the first three months of her life, then, as if trying to make up for the damage she had done to our nervous systems, she set about becoming a perfect child and did a dandy job of it. As the child who always sought to please me, she was my right-hand helper. Her daddy thought she hung the moon. Her teachers called her a perfect student. She grew up believing the whole world loved her because, with the possible exception of her bothersome brothers, it did.

Her smile can still brighten a bad day.

The perfectionistic traits came with a few downsides. Making Casey understand the sky would not fall if she got a B on her grade card was harder than convincing the boys it would not kill them to take a bath every day. Talking to her about the spiritual salvation process was complicated by the fact that, in her early years, she considered herself to be without sin. She claimed she did bad things only because Ben made her do them. Greg and I rather believed her.

Casey developed into a unique combination of characteristics. As a full-grown woman, she stands at barely five feet tall and, on a day without makeup, looks to be about twelve. She loves to read, hates to sweat, and tackles black diamond ski trails. She has a dreadful sense of direction, consistently getting lost when she leaves a restaurant table to go to the bathroom. Yet she spent two years traveling Southeast Asia as a journalist for a missionary organization.

She met her husband, also named Ben, in Thailand and brought him into the family. He cried as she walked down the aisle on the day they got married and I love him a lot.

Micah is the child that most often made me want to tap out of the mother vs. child battle of wills. He had a keen and cunning mind that continually drove me to the frayed end of my parenting rope. He seldom actually crossed the lines of obedience, but he skillfully danced around them until they blurred and crossed. Sometimes they disappeared altogether, and I was left trying to decide if he was standing on the right or wrong side of a line that was no longer there.

When he wasn't dancing all over my last nerve, he was looking for a spotlight and putting on a show. In high school, he developed an endearing quality that drew groups of girls to his light like moths to a flame. While he basked in their attention, they played with his curls and accessorized his hair. Then with the abundance of self-assurance that was born in him, he wore their bows and barrettes to football practice. Micah is funny and witty and always has been our most confident child.

Along with the curly hair I adore, God gave Micah broad shoulders, a giant-sized heart, and the ability to see what others miss. He was the child who came to my rescue when a bad day had beaten me up. He was the elementary student who spoke to the kids standing alone at recess. He was the teenager who took his friends home when they had had too much to drink. Although my second son is strong in many ways, it is his gentleness that makes me most proud.

As an adult, Micah has an impressive job in the corporate arena. He married Melissa and brought her into the family. She guards his heart from the stress of that world, and I love her a lot.

Peter was our happiest child. He sang the most, giggled the best, and took everything in stride. He was most happy when he was playing basketball. You would never have known by looking at him that he was an athlete. He was all skin and bones, and had it not been for the ability to cinch up his pants with the cord in the waist of his uniforms, he would have given his sport fans a different kind of show.

It was Peter whom Greg and I left behind most often. We don't know why. Maybe it is because he was small and easy to misplace. Maybe it is because we subconsciously knew he was the child with the sweetest spirit and the least likely to punish us in our old age for our bevy of parenting mistakes. Either way, I owe his guardian angel a hug of appreciation and a hard high five for a job well done.

Having a fair amount of intelligence, Peter learned from watching the trouble his older brothers brought on themselves with their defiance and manipulation. He decided an impish grin and a cute remark were the best way to convert people to his way of thinking. Armed with those weapons and an ability to dance that amuses and delights, he set out to conquer his little corner of the world. His plan succeeded brilliantly. Everyone loves Peter.

When I first found out my fourth child was a boy, I threw a little hissy fit at God and told him I wanted a girl. He let me know, quietly and firmly, that He was creating that soul for His purposes, not mine. Peter has become a man after the heart of God, a seeker of spiritual things, a lover of grace. I have become a woman captivated by and thankful for the discerning soul and impish grin I thought I didn't want.

Tessa is our baby, our animal lover, our tenderest heart. She has the most color on her fingernails, the most sass in her step, and, by far, the most words on her tongue. When the school day ended for the older kids, they each came home to a chore list. Casey's job was to talk to her sister so I could have a break. (Not kidding about that.) Tessa had so many things to say, she invented friends who would listen to them.

She loved Ashley, Sahka, and Moo. She read them books, told them her best stories, taught them to play follow the leader, and broke up their fights when they all wanted to sit on the floor beside her. We saw Tessa's talent in theatrical arts for the first time when she staged plays with Ashley, Sahka, and Moo as the actors. When she cried real tears with convincing heartbreak because her imaginary friends' imaginary mother died, we knew she was a dramatic prodigy.

Tessa has the heart of an artist. As she got older, we did, indeed, see a dramatic talent develop. When she picked up a ukulele for the first time, we discovered the music. It dances inside her. Sometimes it jitterbugs. Sometimes it sways to a wistful rhythm laid down by her thoughts. Sometimes it leaps and twirls in her own form of worship. When she plays the piano and sings, the music boils up and gushes out of her. In some ways, she is her father's daughter.

Towering over her big sister at 5'8", Tessa has a thick, curly mass of hair that is slightly bigger than a lion's mane. Unfortunately, beneath the hair she also has the head of an artist, mostly clueless about the practicalities of life. In many ways, she is her mother's daughter. Either way, Tessa is our end-of-the-line delight.

I sit in the swing with the man I drove away with on that first day of our life together, and I think about the other things I did not know. I didn't know that when I crawled into my new husband's lap at the end of my work day and laid my head on his chest I would feel I was home. I didn't know the little-boy look in his eyes as he pleaded to watch something dumb on TV would melt me. I didn't know the touch of his hand on my back in a crowd would shelter me, or a tired smile at the end of his work day could make my heartbeat lurch.

As Greg holds my hand, we push our feet against the porch floor and the swing sways.

We have farther to go down our road together, and as I sit here, I wonder where it will take us. I imagine there will be lots more grandchildren Greg and I will try not to leave anywhere. There probably will be more animal incidents, more pans of green beans burned, and more diets begun in the third week of January. For me, there will be more inattention, more procrastination, and more books read when chores are calling for my attention.

Wherever our journey leads us, odds are that I will continue to fall short of the standards set by the Country Seasons Calendar Women hanging on my fridge. But in my failures as a wannabe, I have learned this characteristic of the Virtuous Woman: I am not worried about what is down the road. I am confident God will keep a close eye on me and my family.

And I am certain He will continue with me on the journey. Meeting me in my kitchen. Resting beside me in the porch swing. Speaking through the words of C. S. Lewis. Revealing Himself in music. Surprising me in the blackberry bushes. Dancing with me to the colors of spring.

Let us go on and take the adventures that shall fall to us.
C. S. Lewis, *The Lion, the Witch and the Wardrobe*

Conclusion

Who can find a virtuous woman?
Proverbs 31:10 (KJV)

I realize that before reading this book, some of you didn't know who the Virtuous Woman is. Others of you won't recognize her by my descriptions in these chapters. The pictures of her today are different from those in previous generations. She is stronger now, a warrior referred to as a woman of valor. She no longer wears an apron or vacuums in her pearls. (And I heard a rumor that she had a tailoring come-apart and ran over her sewing machine with a cement mixer.)

In actuality, the woman described in Proverbs 31 is not a real person. That is probably why nobody can find her. She is the compilation of advice about women given to the Bible's King Lemuel by his mother. Her description is written as an acrostic poem. The first letter of each verse in the passage begins with a successive letter of the Hebrew language. With poetic words of wisdom, King Lemuel's mother painted an extraordinary portrait that has been immortalized by Christians as the Virtuous Woman.

As taught to me in the 1970s and into the '80s, she was committed, innovative, enterprising, and perfectly domestic. During that time, I was beginning to search for my identity as a woman of God and found her worth imitating. Touted by traditional Christianity as the epitome of a godly woman, she was a good paradigm by which to model myself.

Although many of my friends wore the Virtuous Woman pattern well, it didn't much fit me. Because I thought it would please God, I worked hard to shape myself around it. Day after day I stuffed myself into the mold. But the part of me that wasn't domestic and didn't remember to pick up my kids and couldn't commit to a consistent quiet time kept popping out in places. Again and again I hid those inadequacies from the church world because I was sure that adherence to the pattern was expected of me.

But as I got older, the mold began to bind me. The constraints of the Proverbs 31 woman as they were taught to me tightened until my soul had trouble breathing inside them. At some point I gave up and stopped the struggle.

I'm not sure how it happened. I wish I could say I gained the courage to break out of the mold. But it would be ridiculous to think I had that much confidence in myself. I think, maybe, the Holy Spirit simply showed up outside the lines of the pattern and held out His hand. He drew me away from a set of good and worthy lifestyle choices that were never intended to be mine and put me on a different path to life with God, a path He had carved just for me.

I used to try to impress God with long, profound prayers. But my mind tended to wander off before my mouth was through. It was more pointless than profound. He never wanted me to pray with eloquence. He created someone else to do that. All I need is one word. He gave me the understanding that one word uttered goes straight to the throne of God.

I've tried to discipline myself to keep a scheduled quiet time, but I have never succeeded. Instead, I open the Bible in irregular bursts of intense research. And He speaks to me in its pages.

God loves committed, innovative, enterprising, and perfectly domestic women. He created a bunch of them. But I'm not one. I am a procrastinating, inattentive, indecisive, domestically challenged woman who sees God in the color of the sky and the force of a storm. I am also a contemplative and creative woman who sends Him abounding gratitude in the spring when the trees begin to bloom, who prays in church with her eyes open, and who worships with words she writes because, although she can carry a tune, she can't keep it in only one key.

Now that you have read to the end of this book, you probably realize it isn't really about the Virtuous Woman. I wrote it to put into words what I discovered about God and me during the years I tried to emulate her. My Virtuous Woman Wannabe tales come to an end with a very simple understanding.

Not only does God love me, He also likes me.

DAY LANDS!

He likes the procrastinating, inattentive, indecisive, domestically challenged me. After all, He created me this way when He sat with His tongue between His teeth and intricately formed my soul.

There is one thing I alone can give to God. It is the unique relationship that only He and I can have. When I stopped trying to force myself into someone else's mold, I was free to give it to Him.

And He began to enjoy me as He created me to be.

I'm pretty sure He likes you too. You should ask Him about that.

Acknowledgments

When God sat down with His tongue between His teeth and created my soul, He gave me the ability to write stories. He did not give me the organizational skills or self-confidence to take those stories and turn them into a book. Instead, He sent me a wonderful group of people to help with that.

My husband's confidence in my ability to write never waivers. He is positive that you, your mom, your great-aunt Sissy, your neighbor on the corner, and the lady who does your nails down at the salon will all love this book. He was the motivating force behind this project and is my greatest encouragement to write about the humor in our lives.

When I first began to write about my kids, I worried that they would be embarrassed by the stories and ask me to stop. Instead, they counted the number of sentences I used to describe each of them and held me accountable for keeping them even. My children like to be appear in my tales. They give me complete freedom to write about the humor in our lives.

The women God put in my path over the years gave inspiration to many of the thoughts I wrote here. Some of them mothered me. Some mentored me. Some talk and laugh and do life with me. A few of them show up in these pages. All of them are part of my heart's story. They will be the first to click their computer mice and buy this book.

When I finished the first draft of this manuscript, I asked 40 people to read through it. When they logged in to be my reading group, the project became more than mine. They gave me ten weeks of their time, insights and suggestions that smoothed the rough edges from the work, and the encouragement I needed to complete the book.

Erin Brown (The Write Editor) edited the manuscript and Jeff Beck (graphic designer) designed the cover. They were the only two people on the project who actually knew what they were doing. They patiently led me through the process of publishing this book and never led me to believe they were rolling their eyes or shaking their heads on the other side of the computer screen.

Without this list of people, my VWW tales never would have been published. If I was a true Virtuous Woman, I would bake them all a chocolate pie. But that ship never reached port. Instead, I give them my thanks and profound appreciation.

Contact the Author

These are my stories. They are tales of my life as a young wife and mother and the accounts of my experiences with God along the way.

I hope they made you laugh. I hope they also encouraged you to chill a little and rest in the fact that God doesn't expect you to meet a standard in order to please Him.

Our stories about life with God are the most precious things we have to offer the world. I would love to hear a bit of yours.

You can contact me at *lanorthcuttwrites@gmail.com* .

You can read more of my stories and God thoughts on my website. You can also see pictures of the people and events in these pages. Visit me there at *lanorthcutt.com.*

Permissions

Scripture quotations marked ASV are taken from the American Standard Version. (Public Domain.) Scripture quotations marked DBT are taken from the Darby Translation Bible (Public Domain). Scripture quotations marked ESV are taken from the ESV® Bible (The Holy Bible, English Standard Version®), copyright © 2001 by Crossway, a publishing ministry of Good News Publishers. Used by permission. All rights reserved. Scripture quotations marked GW are taken from GOD'S WORD, a copyrighted work of God's Word to the Nations. Quotations are used by permission. Copyright 1995 by God's Word to the Nations. All rights reserved. Scripture quotations marked ISV are taken from *The Holy Bible: International Standard Version.* Release 2.0, Build 2015.02.09. Copyright © 1995-2014 by ISV Foundation. ALL RIGHTS RESERVED INTERNATIONALLY. Used by permission of Davidson Press, LLC. Scripture quotations marked KJV are taken from the King James Version of the Bible. (Public Domain.) Scripture quotations marked TLB are taken from The Living Bible, copyright © 1971. Used by permission of Tyndale House Publishers, Inc., Carol Stream, Illinois 60188. All rights reserved. Scripture quotations marked NASB are taken from the New American Standard Bible®, copyright ©1960, 1995 by The Lockman Foundation. Used by permission. (www.Lockman.org). Scripture quotations marked NLT are taken from the Holy Bible, New Living Translation, copyright ©1996, 2007 by Tyndale House Foundation. Used by permission of Tyndale House Publishers, Inc., Carol Stream, Illinois 60188. Scripture quotations marked GNT are taken from the Good News Translation in Today's English Version—Second Edition. Copyright © 1992 by American Bible Society. Used by permission. Scripture quotations marked THE MESSAGE are taken from THE MESSAGE. Copyright © by Eugene H. Peterson 1993, 2002. Used by permission of NavPress.

All rights reserved. Represented by Tyndale House Publishers, Inc.

28586510R00092

Made in the USA
Lexington, KY
19 January 2019